DEDICATED TO

MY GRANDCHILDREN
AND THEIR PARENTS

D0988696

IN LOVING MEMORY

MILDRED CARTER
WARREN "SWEDE" JONNSON
JOHN & DORTHY ZUCK

ISBN 0-9613657-9-X

STOOPS PUBLISHING
10 North Elliott Avenue
Aurora MO.   65605

FRONT COVER: Nickie Carter, Winner of National Air Races
Cleveland OH, 8-31-47

THIS IS NICKIE CARTER

"AN obsession can become the limit of your horizon. The world of flying is like the music world, or the arts; it twines around your heartstrings, becomes a way of life that leaves room for nothing else love, marriage, family, even spiritual integrity--if you let it. I know. I did it."

Nickie Carter, famed American aviatrix, earned her pilot's license at sixteen. She was one of the 1,073 heroines who ferried warplanes for the Air Force during World War. She won the United States air race championship for woman pilots. She founded a flying school to train illustrious pilots. So far as Nickie Carter was concerned the human spirit could soar no higher than the wings of man canreach.

Then a knock on the door and a tall patient lady entered her life to point out that the Creator made male and female to image Him. That opened a grander horizon---the challenge to reflect Him in His Love, Wisdom, Justice and her own personality. Would that challenge conflict with flying? No. It would conflict with prioities.

Swede, her husband, recognized the tall lady's message as the truth that frees the soul. But under test it proved to Nickie Carter to be "a song of sensuous loves", beautiful but not for real. Spurred by indomitable willpower, she sacrificed marriage and family, even spiritual values, to maintain flying schools and establish international ailines.

Her downfall came from entanglements with Government bureaucracies. For years Carter was hounded by the FBI, finally arrested, brought to trial, and sentenced to five years in Federal prison. The judge-rescinded.the-conviction,however, as it was on a specious charge.

But then there came the sentence from a higher court. What do you do when conscience shackles you and leads you to the day of reckoning? Can inflexible self-will bend before breaking and learn Godly humility? What can quench hate and vexation in a bitter soul? She had defied the superior authorities of the state and congregational elders alike.

"I don't want to be a rebel," Nickie Carter finally decided. "I'm not out to prove I'm a liberated femalried that. She ended up being dominated by a spineless man."

How hard the return of the prodigal daughter. She was disfellowshiped twice from her faith, to the despair of her family and the friends who tried to help her. GRAND HORIZON recounts one remarkable woman's struggle to overcome the tragedies of deeply entrenched traits. This is the Nickie Carter story.

"This world is the limit of their horizon."
THE BIBLE, Philippians 3:20, PHILLIPS TRANSLATION

GRAND HORIZON

DAUGHTERS OF FIFINELLI

EMPTY NEST

JOY and DESPAIR

BANISHED

NEW HORIZON

DAUGHTERS

OF

FIFINELLI

W.A.S.P.

WOMEN AIR FORCE SERVICE PILOTS WW II

Chapter 1

"GIVE ME WINGS!"

WE were the hottest roller derby queens in the League. Our names glittered on the Rollerdome marquee:

NICKIE CARTER

KERRY MEYER

In that order. How important it was to me that you know that! Kerry saw the same vision. But in reverse order. Of course.

We meant it. About being roller derby queens. I don't remember how we gulled our Moms into allowing us a whole day's bike excursion. We were tough cookies, wiry as hickory withes, and they knew that. We could peddle for twelve hours and still take on our brothers on the softball court. What we didn't tell them was that we were bound for Cleveland. Ninety long miles from Clyde, Ohio.

We pedaled and we pedaled. We'd pause at a roadside park to steam. Then on we'd go. Once we stopped for lunch. Lunch was a can of beans. Only dumb Kerry neglected the can opener. We stomped on the can. We ran and jumped on it. Finally it squirted beans on a tree and on my socks. We salvaged what we could.

Pedaling down the streets of Cleveland was not like pedaling down the two traffic lights of Clyde. After a lot of stops and retracing we located the Rollerdome on Euclid Avenue.

We offloaded our skates and started up the ramp and found the stairs. Through the auditorium and down into the pits. It was awesome. Some of the teams were there, taking a break and passing a lot of rough banter, coarse and mean, like we'd expect from our heroines. Star struck kids like us must have been a common sight. They'd point and razz us. One big hairy ape of a female waved. "Hey, Pee-Wees, wanta try bumpsa Daisy with little ole me?"

You let bullies like that know where to get off. "Oversized buffalo!" I shook a fist at her, "How'd you get your start?"

I got a roar of ovation. The buffalo started for me. "On your duffer, Tiny!" a man yelled, and this tall guy with a mustache like a bow tie got in front of her and stepped toward us. I recognized him as Gus the team manager from the newspapers.

"What're you kids doing here?"

"Where do we sign up?" I demanded.

That brought the house down all over again. Only this time they were laughing. Gus saw what it did to us. "Look," he said, not unkindly, "this is one tough racket. You wouldn't last two seconds."

No amount of telling him how we both survived among brothers, beaten and slammed every day, nothing stopped Gus from shaking his head.

"I don't raise my girls. I just train them. One thing I don't want," Gus shouted over the furor, "is mamas on my neck."

That cut to the heart. Gus' last words trailed off in our ears. "Come back in five years. Maybe I'll give you a tryout."

Five years was four years beyond eternity . Kerry sniffed. "They don't care about nobody." WE needed a sanctum where we could try to recover. I said, "Let's go back to that airport and watch the planes."

Feeling forlorn and misbegotten we pedaled haphazardly through a maze of taxis and streetcars and glares. It was a long, lonely way from home.

Through the main gateway of Cleveland Municipal Airport and past the flight school signs; then we stopped by a school called Aeroways. Little did I dream that years later I would be readying to win the Cleveland National Air Races and international fame from this very hangar.

A smiley young guy came out and grinned at us. "Hiah," he said. "I'm Joe." he would have shooed us off, but then he saw the dried tear channels down our cheeks. "Uh-oh," he said. Then he paused. "Uh, would you two young ladies like to learn to fly?"

"You mean it?" I said. "How much does it cost?"

Joe drew a circle with his toe. "Four hundred dollars."

Four hundred dollars minus $3.28, the balance from my paper route. I didn't even answer.

2

Joe pointed to an airplane. "See that Meyer? I'm taking 'er up for a test flight. Wanta try it out? No charge."

"You mean it?" I was on my feet in a flash.

"Nickie, you crazy?" Kerry couldn't believe it. "He says it's a test flight. Don't you know what that means? It ain't even been off the ground before!"

"I don't care!" I said. "I wanta go up there and spit on the Rollerdome."

Joe told us to bring our bikes and gear inside the chain fence, all the time Kerry begging me not to be an idiot. Joe showed me how to get into the parachute and get the seat belt snugged up. I felt packaged for air delivery. This ought to tell you how far back in the age of innocence we lived. A licensed pilot instructor takes a 16-year-old kid off the street on a test flight---who is she? parental permission? insurance?---not one word on a dotted line.

Joe got someone to spin the prop. We started taxying out. Cleveland Municipal was different in those days; no radio tower for little planes. They had their own section for take-off and landing.

That wide, salivary grin I was to know so well , was fixed on Joe's face.

We took off. I waved at Kerry, a lonesome little figure, her face in her hands, receding away behind us. Then the glorious, terrifying lift-off and leaving the earth far and farther below. We climbed. I felt an exhilaration I have never been able to put into words, an enlivening of the spirit, a mending of the heart, a leaving behind of all that ever hurt you, or ever mattered. We spiraled into what seemed glorious heights (probably 3,000 feet) into a different world, a world only wings could bring you to. Joe turned and looked back, still grinning. "Seat belt fastened? I' gonna check 'er out now."

I nodded vigorously. He pulled up the nose. The plane seemed to hang on nothing. All of a sudden it veered off to my left and my whole inner being felt as if left back there. Then I was looking straight down at a road far below and spinning round and round...Then whammo the nose stopped spinning and we pulled out. A ton of wind was pushing me back into the seat. The grin again---"You like that?" The wind was lashing my face with tears.

"Oh boy!" I screamed. "We climbed high in the sky, outbounding the horizon. This time he pointed the nose down at a thin thread of road, roaring for speed and we hurtled earthward. I lost my senses between life and death. Then a ponderous shaking of every strut and rivet, then up, up and over, upside-down and back downhill towards the road---"That was a loop!" Joe shouted. We spun. We looped some more. We stalled. We wing-overed until Joe got so tired he grinned dry- mouthed. He headed for the airport. We entered the pattern, floated down and landed, and taxied back to Aeroways. Joe helped me disembark. Kerry ran up, utterly astounded to find me alive.

"Boy, oh boy oh boy!" I grabbed her, prancing circles around her. "Nothing else in this world I want to do but fly---Give me wings!"

NICKIE AND MEYER PLANE
THE TYPE JOE GAVE HER THE FIRST PLANE RIDE IN

Chapter 2

CLOUD NINE

MOM was a cynical woman. A widow, life had bitten her hard and she had bitten it back. She never went to church. "God's not there, she'd say. "Why bother?"

Still, as though just to be sure, she did send me and my two brothers to Methodist Sunday School---"To learn the basics of God, anyhow." But when she learned that one of the "basics" we were being taught was that God frenchfries hapless sinners in hellfire she wondered if maybe we ought to join the no-hellers. We always wondered just what she had in mind. My brother Don and I had a problem of our own. We had to pass the candy store on Main Street on our way to Sunday School. The problem was which to choose. Our nickels seldom if ever reached their intended destination, the collection plate.

Me, I never had a problem believing in a supreme being. I loved nature, being raised on the edge of a woods. I loved animals. And birds. Especially birds. Some power vastly beyond man had to create feathered bodies with wings.

As for Sunday School, the basics of God were confusing. There was the mystery of the Trinity. And the nature-loving God who created beautiful birds frenchfried humans in hell-fire forever. It didn't jibe with something I picked up somewhere, whether from Mom or Sunday School, but something in the Bible about an eye for an eye, a life for a life---a matter of equal justice. Like for like. If you end a life then your own life should end. But if you end a life and are tortured forever for it, does that not go beyond like for like, 'way beyond equal justice? Mom, in her angriest moment would not go to such devilish extremes with us kids. But wouldn't God, with so much more patience and endurance than Mom, bless her soul, wouldn't He abide by his own rule of equal justice? As I say, the basics were confusing.

5

way. Still shattered by those roller derby dinks. She swore off from watching a roller derby ever again. After my frolic in the clouds with Smiling Joe I couldn't have cared less. "Roller derby? What an earthbound *illusion*!" I pitied her and told her so. It practically destroyed a friendship. We didn't speak for the last forty miles.

What I was grappling with in my mind was how to manage this ordeal with Mom. I must leave home. No way of getting around it. Positively none.

Mom came home Monday evening in the right mood. The mood to be victimized. That is, tired and weary, with no fight left. Raising two sons and a daughter through the Great Depression was something other than heaven on earth. We all pitched in and helped. I had delivered newspapers on the streets at five, and worked up a route which I kept through school years.

As I say, she came home vulnerable Monday night. I always timed the Big Ones for the moment when she was lowest.

"Mom, I've got to get a better job!" I popped both fists on my kneecaps vehemently. "Can't stand to see you come home like this every night."

"Oh?" She didn't try to hide her suspicion. Still she appreciated that somebody cared.

"A girl my age, still nothing but a paper route? It's for the birds! Ab-so-lutely!" I shouldn't have said birds. That brought the thought of wings. Wings made my eyes pop.

She saw it. She sipped her coffee, her eyes pinned on me. She leaned her head back on her purple cushion. Waiting. How I hated it when she just sat back, looked at me, and waited.

"I've got to get a better job, that's all! And you know I can't get anything decent in Clyde, Ohio!"

She drew a long breath that kind of lifted her shoulders. But that was all.

"So I've got to go to Cleveland. I've got to get a real job."

I knew she would let me listen back to my own words and digest them.

Finally she said, quietly: "You're sixteen, aren't you?"

"Goin' on seventeen!" I said sharply. "I'll be seventeen before you know it."

Before the week was out I was on my way to Cleveland.

I FOUND a room to fit my meager budget. I trudged the streets. Two weeks I walked those streets, and that last day when I was debating whether to kill myself or call Mom, I found it. File clerk at General Motors, Diesel Division. Defense projects. The pay was good. Many, many hours of overtime. I worked hard and long. Not only could I send money home. As soon as I had saved a few hundred dollars I was off to Aeroways and Smiling Joe. I plunked my money down. An hour later off I went into the blue for my first lesson!

I lived at the airport when I was not working. Evenings I went out with Joe and the airport crowd. Talk was totally about flying and the big events of the day.

I took my ground school courses next door to Sky Tech. My circle of friends expanded. For me there was no other world. I stashed the roller skates in the back of the closet. Stacks of books and papers on meteorology and navigation and the like spilled all over my room.

It was in Ground School , there at Sky Tech, that I met Swede. He was taking an aircraft maintenance course as well as learning to fly. He told me while we were having a drink at the Snake Pit across the street that he had signed up for the Air Force Cadets. He was waiting for his training call. Talk about a lousy stroke---why couldn't I have been one of my brothers and one of my brothers have been a girl! Here Swede was off to the Air Force to train and fly all those magnificent military planes, the P39's and P40's. He'd say he got a thrill just refueling them.

While we were sitting there that day, December 7, 1941, the radio blasted the news---the Japanese attacked Pearl Harbor.

Within the week Swede was called. I went with him to the railroad station. He was reporting for duty in Mississippi. I promised to write him. He gave me a good luck token, a soldier doll he called *Djigooblie*. *Djigooblie* was some kind of mythological imp that became a cupid. It wouldn't have surprised me to know that I would marry this cadet, Swede, better known as Warren

7

Johnson. That's how frivolously lifetime commitments of the young and not so young are all too often made. Never did I dream that I would make his life miserable because of my first love, Wings.

MY TRAINING advanced. I advanced out of sheer intensity. Joe said I was a natural born pilot. I could hardly wait to get to the airport after work, and I only worked overtime enough from this point on to pay for my lessons and send Mom a little now and then.

One day, while taking a break, I picked up a *Readers Digest.* What caught my eye was this article about a flying club operated by Piper Aircraft in Lock Haven, Pennsylvania. Workers, welders, sheet metal workers or whatever, could fly for $1.12 an hour in the Piper Aircraft. I wrote a letter for information and enclosed my application for a job.

The war involvement reached fever pitch following Pearl Harbor. Both coasts discontinued pleasure flying and aviation buffs were converted to military aspirants. Wow, a boy sure had the advantages. Joe broke the news to me at Cleveland Airport: No more flying except for defense. I took it like a death blow.

I called the Piper Factory. And that brought a resurrection. I had qualified as a welding trainee. Come to Lock Haven PA.

I gave my boss zero notice. I rushed to pack my flying gear, pants and shirts. Joe took me to the railroad station. Smiling Joe bid me good-by, a tear in his eye for a favorite student. And I had one for my favorite instructor.

At Lock Haven I was hired as a sheet metal worker. I worried some that welding might be hard on my eyes and interfere with my flying career. "Don't worry," Shirley, a fellow worker, reassured me. Shirley shared my enthusiasm for flying. Right away she became my roommate.

I came to know well---too well---how Pipers were put together, and it somewhat shattered my illusions that airplanes, like people, are slightly less than perfect.

Flying at Lock Haven was somewhat curtailed. Snow was deep that winter.   In the spring the Susquehanna River overflowed its banks. The airport on the shore was submerged. We had the thrill of flying some of the planes to higher ground. Then, because of the fact there were many more students than aircraft and instructors, the favorite way to cut down the scheduling was to ground students on any pretext for a week or two. I stayed grounded and choleric a lot of the time.

Then came the day.

"Listen to this, Shirley", I broke in, in the middle of lunch, "It says here that Jacqueline Cochran is starting WAFS--- gals ferrying warplanes. She's hoping to expand the Air Force with the help of General Hap Arnold." The WAFS,   it appeared , would be used by the military to ferry planes or for other flight duty.

Let me do some explaining about Miss Jacqueline Cochran She was simply the most famous pilot of the twentieth century. Or so The Womens Air Force Service Pilots said, in those very words. She was pioneering womens lib in aviation by hassling the airlines to give her a job piloting a big liner. By 1941 she was leading volunteer women pilots in ferrying planes in England to free men pilots. Then after Pearl Harbor the United States got involved. Jacqueline proposed to General Henry (Hap) Arnold to start a similar program in the United States. Women pilots here, like in England, would free men flyers for overseas duty. By September Miss Cochran was home from England to put her plan to work. That's what I was filling in Shirley about. Within two years the *WASPs* (Womens Air Force Service Pilots) would be ferrying aircraft from factories to military bases all over the States, and even ferrying some fighters across the Atlantic.

"Wow!" Shirley responded with her one word for wonders great and small. "How do we qualify?"

That was vague. "It seems that mainly you have to be interviewed by her highness, Miss Jacqueline Cochran, in person."

Jackie, as they called her, had a cosmetic factory in New York which didn't seem to involve a lot of her time. So far, according to what I was reading, she had only some 25 women pilots qualified to ferry aircraft, planes of two-to-four-engine bomber types.

Was it possible that the mythical superwoman might actually be contacted at her cosmetics company in New York? Shirley and I looked at each other, each one trying to draw the longer breath. "You call her," Shirley whispered.

Serendipity. Within the week Shirley and I were on the train for the Big City and a date with Her Highness.

We got off at Grand Central Station. Talk about a couple of green hicks. We got a very modest room on Times Square. Next day we prepared for the Big One.

We put on our hot pilot togs. We actually turned heads---maybe for looking so corny---and wound up our way to Miss Cochran's headquarters. In the lobby we stopped breathing and just gawked at the compass design in the tile. The pictures of the famed flyer, the surroundings, the very air we breathed, everything was awesome.

Time came when we were ushered into the Presence. We stood there, legs akimbo and speechless. She arose in that sharp blue uniform and looked us over and commenced to shake her head.

"You're going to be disappointed," she said. "It's your height . I mean your lack of it."

I was five feet two. Shirley was maybe half an inch taller. "You're two short to reach the rudders on big pursuit planes," Her Highness was saying. "You'll never qualify for more than flight instructors."

"No matter," we told her frantically. "All we want is to fly for you. We'll accept any duty" She looked straight at us, knowing we were lying and that we'd find some way to grow an inch, even if we had to have our legs stretched.

"All right then," she compromised. And then she actually said, as she shook hands with us, "You'll get a letter with your assignment date for Sweetwater,Texas, in the next two weeks."

How we constrained ourselves till we were on the street, I don't know. We left our idol's presence, telling each other she said it, she really did. We had to celebrate by splurging in Times Square on Singapore Slings.

Our report date came through the mail, just as she promised. We left a few days early to go home and say good-by to our folks. We would meet in Sweetwater, Shirley and I.

Mom was overcome with pride mixed with misgivings. "I told you I don't want you flying those airplanes, Nickie. It's too dangerous. But you never would listen to me." Then she glowed. Her daughter was going to be connected in some important way with the United States Air Force. It made a splash in the Clyde Enterprise.

I routed through Mississippi to see my *Djigooblie* Swede. What a reception! When the officers at Kessler Air Force Base found out I was going to be one of Jacqueline Cochran's gals, they called Swede off duty to the office. He came in looking real nervous, wondering if the jig was up. That's when he first saw me. His officer gave him the day off.

We went to town and celebrated. We had a couple evenings to compare notes. I watched him march. He told his buddies his girlfriend was in the stands and she was on her way to Sweetwater for the same cadet training. As they passed me they gave a special salute. To say I felt anything less than iridescent is understanding it ingloriously. Shirley and I would be parading in the same style.

I said good-by to my cadet with a wistful heartache. For all we knew it might be our last good-by. But---is it really anybody's business but mine?---I felt a compensating joy when I boarded that train for Sweetwater.

That train ride seemed like two miles forward, three miles backward, taking on soldiers at every cowshed. The nation like the rest of the world was at war. The train overflowed with heaving, grunting bodies, with luggage stacked in the aisles. Most of the guys were anything but thrilled about their assignments. Nobody was as thrilled as I was about mine.

A little sweaty, dusty town was Sweetwater, Texas. But to me it was Joysville. I would spend nine exhilarating months at Avenger Field, as the base was called.

I recall vaguely that a handful of "religious fanatics" were being hounded out of town for refusing military service and declaring "wars and rumors of wars" were a sure sign of the last days. There was noise in the newspapers about some mob trying to hang a man for claiming to be neutral, but the rope broke. Not that I gave any attention to, other than to scorn the idea that anybody could be so out of harmony with the spirit of the times that he could not appreciate the holiness of our cause.

Chapter 3

SWEETWATER'S ANGELS

STEPPING off the train in Sweetwater TX was the beginning of one of the most memorable periods of my young and willful life, the beginning of the fulfillment of a dream. By dream I mean not some idle "Wouldn't it be nice" notion that drifts through your reveries, too out of reach for you to make the remotest effort to go after. I mean the kind of dream that haunts you in your sleep as well as in your waking hours---a driving force that never lets you rest, an all consuming kind of obsession, an ignition that lights you up for all the world to see or burns you to a cinder and nobody much is aware that you even passed from the land of the living.

Not many seventeen-year-olds in my generation had such an opportunity.

It amounted to a $70,000 education in aviation by Uncle Sam and the privilege of flying around this grand and glorious country. I paid secret homage to my benefactress Jacqueline Cochran. Whatever God I believed in, I thanked him that she was a woman. She, in fact, was nearer to me than God, coming closer to being God than any worshipful being on my horizon.

As I taxied through the town of Sweetwater I loved every brick in every building. We passed City Hall where later there would stand the statue of Fifinella, the *WASP* insignia created out of a mythological figure by Walt Disney. There she stands today, the little cherub in boots, wings and goggles, and her wings spread. Goddess of the *WASPs*.

Avenger Field was, to me, a delight---the barracks, the recreation hall (who needed that with flying?), the administration buildings, and, ah, best of all, the military hangars sheltering the PT l9 Fairchild's, the basic trainers, the advanced trainers, the T-6 and wow, a twin engine Cessna today known as the Bamboo of each of them. Mind you, today they're all museum relics, but in the '40s they were state of the art in trainer aviation. To me this was heaven opened up.

I met my "roomies" and what a rainbow of personalities! We nicknamed ourselves after the seven dwarfs. Flower was tall and demure and very quiet. Thumper was to become my special buddy, maybe because she was only five feet tall. If goddess of wings Cochran was right, that we shorties would never be ferry pilots, then Thumper would be by my side. I was Twitter, because I was ecstatic about the whole prospect of flying, and some even said, in a complimentary way, a non-complainer, or maybe too dumb to complain---anyway, a rarity or oddity in a military barracks. Thumper made up for that. She must have been born complaining. She was a more seasoned pilot, already instructing pilots, so felt entitled to gripe about everything and everybody. We were opposites to the nth degree.

The first day we five rookies were hazed unmercifully by the upper class. We had to scrub our barracks, remake our beds a zillion times, shine shoes, then shine the polish on the shoes. Thumper griped her head off. Twitter grinned like a nut.

THE TRUTH is, the Training Detachment at Avenger Field was not a paradise. One magazine described it as a place so remote it made Houston look like a vacation resort. Let me read you what it said: "The field was at Sweetwater, Texas, a bleak and arid place where nothing grows but mesquite trees and buffalo grass." Half the time we were flying through dust storms, it said, and the summers were so hot the gals in cockpits had to shed their blouses and bras. We were under strict military regimen with men in charge.

Let me explain a bit here. We were not strictly Air Force cadettes, though treated or mistreated as though we were. As I'll explain later, it took almost four decades of shilly-shally and an act of Congress before the Air Force adopted us officially. Anyway, we got the same training as cadets. We liked to think we were on a par with any male.

But talk about chauvinism. Wow was it there! I don't mean just at training center. It was anywhere and everywhere a woman tried to intrude her way into the sanctum of male dominated aviation. And harassment? That's where modern Tailhook scandals were born and bred. When Jacqueline Carter offered to ferry a bomber across the Atlantic, to prove a woman could do it as well as a man, she ran head-on into the rankest humiliation. One aeronautics magazine described it this way:

"Everything seemed to be on schedule, when at the last moment the male pilots threatened to strike if the flight were undertaken. Military flying was considered a sacrosanct male preserve, and the assignment of women to such work would tend to downgrade their male status as pilots. Finally, under a compromise, Cochran agreed to fly the bomber across the Atlantic, but she would have to give up controls to her male copilot on takeoff and landing." Talk about gall....

In some ways most of us were oblivious to this sort of thing at Avenger Field. At evening after taps we gals in our barracks got so we'd expect as a matter of course to hear a knocking on our window. In the barracks next to ours were the male cadets. Sweetwater was still co-educational. Time came when we had the boys waiting on us like servants. They'd bring us tidbits from the mess hall, which we'd scorn. We had them sneaking into town nine miles away to bring us hamburgers. We'd open the barracks window long enough to snatch the goodies, then slammo. We were not messing around to ruin our golden prospects. All the gals had their heads in the stars, but not about guys. The cadets were so happy to have females that close to look at and to serve and to dream about the times when there were girls in their lives.

Not only were cadets off limits, but, most of all, it was pointed out to us, most of all were the flight instructors off limits. No chance for bribery. That, of course, became our secret delight and prize, to have a sneak date with an instructor on an off-duty weekend. Some of the gals ended up after the war marrying their favorite instructors.

15

The instructor, to me, existed somewhere in that ethereal region not far from Jacqueline Cochran. He could teach me all I wanted to know about the flying machines. That was my thrill. I wanted to fly, fly, fly.

Some of the gals, those with more bucks, and the older, more seasoned pilots, would rent cabins at Lake Sweetwater. That was the "in" place, the place to have parties and invite instructors. Taxies would deliver the off-limit booze.

My little group was a lot less affluent. Our thrill was the Sweetwater drugstore on Saturday night. Cadets from nearby Big Springs would bus over. They'd buy a little bathroom gin and we'd invade the drugstore and sit and imbibe. Probably we'd end up in the local upstairs dance hall.

The dear people of Sweetwater, in an effort to keep us from getting homesick, would invite us to their homes. I never saw a homesick gal while I was there, not even Thumper. They'd wrap us in that patriotic closeness that goes with a war, and make heroines out of us. The only time a tear was shed was when a gal washed out from training and said good-by to Avenger Field.

THE primary trainers, the PT Fairchild's, were a delight---open air cockpits, the whole feeling, goggles, zuitsuits, and parachutes. Our flight suit issue was cadet coveralls. Since we were the first females in this man's air force, needless to say they were oversized. Poor Thumper looked as though she'd crawled up the legs and into hers, and was always in a quandary trying to find her way out. We got some camera shots of this regalia that made *Life* magazine.

Our adventures kept the Sweetwater *Gazette* loaded with items. One gal was attempting the slow rolls the instructor was teaching her. She forgot one detail, to buckle her seatbelt. When the plane rolled she parted company. She landed in Sweetwater Lake and the plane in a nearby field.

Then there was Sue, our cross-country champion. She was perfect except for timing. Three times on here cross country solo she flew right over Sweetwater at 5,000 feet. She'd phone her instructor from some other airport. He'd guide her back and over Sweetwater she'd go again to some other landing. Everything and every town in West Texas looks alike from the air. Figuring arrival time is the quintessential. On her last attempt over, they sent up a barrage of circling PT's at 5,000 feet as an airmark.

The big tension on the flight line was when your name came up on the flight blackboard for a check ride. Two pink slips and out of the wild blue yonder you'd go. Nothing could describe the heartbreak when a *WASP* trudged from the ready room after a washout to pack her bags. I watched my friend Shirley from Piper Factory days take that walk. I would not have felt worse at her funeral. The instructors, trying to be kind, always used the worst words possible---"It's for your own good---You'll find something else to do...."

They might as well have advised to get married or commit suicide. There were 1,830 women admitted to the *WASP* program; 756 were rejected.

I got one pink slip. It was like some Armageddon I'd heard about. Twitter stopped twittering. Nothing any longer to grin about. Nothing but mortal dread. Dread of being banished--- maybe to Clyde,Ohio.

The second check ride is indescribably worse, at least during the anticipation period---that horrible tension of *knowing* it's now or never. This devil of an instructor has a prospect lined up for washout---you. In your imagination he's like a cop scribbling tickets. I was sitting in the airplane on my parachute, waiting for my check pilot to come out, trying to pray to God or Fifinella or somebody, telling myself, "Nickie Carter, you must remain *relaxed* or coordination will be shot and you might as well jump out of the plane."

The fear that paralyzed me was this particular instructor. His very name was Ogre. Corporal Ogre. To his back we called him The Oag. It was The Oag's policy to treat us like men---this is one case in which we didn't like it---severe tongue lashings and all the coarseness that went with it. We could take it or take off, a thing he knew we'd never do, willingly. At one time in training he told me to do a power-over stall and then some coordinated turns. After half an hour of shouted abuse I tore off my helmet and earphones, throttled back to quiet the engine and stuck my head out of the cockpit and shouted back at him, "Stop being so (deleted) smart! I'm doing the best I can." Oag quieted. Just to bide his time. His time was now.

I mounted my parachute and buckled the seat belt and sweated blood. Then out pops this other pilot and hops in and says in a most congenial way, "Start 'er up and let's be off!"

I have no recollection whatsoever of taxying out and taking off. Amnesia slipped away up there in the clouds and I was flying like a swan, up and down and around with velvety ease. I knew I had made it. Back we went to the Avenger. He hopped out and actually salute "Thanks for the ride. You passed!"
Near fainting I heard him critiquing me a bit on small points. He turned to leave. That's when Corporal Ogre came out. In a rage.

"Why'd you take my student---That's my schedule!"My guy saluted, then bowed. "I simply took the wrong plane."

SWEDE called. He proposed. He wanted to be my flight instructor forever. Nothing could be more wonderful. In the euphoria of the moment I said Yes.

NICKIE,ZOOTSUIT & PT FAIRCHILD

NICKIE,GEAR & BT VULTEE (vibrator)

NICKIE CARTER IN NEW UNIFORM

JACQUELINE COCHRAN (left)
SWEETWATER TX

Chapter 4

THE VULTEE VIBRATOR

OUR next step after graduating from the pretty PT's was the BT (Basic Training) better known as the ugly duckling Vultee Vibrator. To us it was a giant among aircraft. So big we climbed up and on the wing and into the cockpit, and that was a struggle. Thumper and I needed five pillows besides our parachutes to keep from looking like kids sunk in a bathtub.

While continuing our cross-country work, we started into instrument training in the BT. How can I describe instrument work at that stage of its evolution? The student sits in the back seat, the instructor in the front. You pull a lever and a big tentlike canopy comes over your head. It is hard to see with the little tube like florescence. All this adds to trying to fly a radio range which was the big thing then. You go by sound only. Dit-dat and dat-dit. When the dit-dat and the dat-dit run together you are on course.

While listening for this magic code you are trying all the while to balance the lumbering vibrator with needle ball and airspeed only. Amidst the vibration of the airplane, and the noise of the engine, and keeping the needle in place, and the ball centered, and trying to make out a dit-dat from a dat-dit,---*and* trying to decipher a complicated range homing problem two minutes out---was the l80 degree turn across the beam a false leg, or true?---add to this a little rough Texas summer air, and your instructor yelling "What the (delete) are you doin' back there?" in the intercom...can you make sense out of what I'm saying? That's how far high tech had to catch up with instrument flying.

As I sit back in my aerocommander today and punch in the automatic pilot coupled to the simplified VOR range, and let everything take place by itself, I marvel over and over again how any of us survived an actual instrument flight. Especially when you got in a real storm and were bouncing all over the sky. You were an unsung hero to fly the plane on the quietest day of the year. At that time the radio always became deafening with static. It was practically impossible to detect a Morse code underneath the blast.*

Night flying was another adventure, the very horror of the instructors. It was beautiful, at least, under the stars of Texas. Not that we were up there to marvel at how the lights of heaven bestowed a soft radiance over bleak western plains. We were up there to learn about vertigo, what it is, what it is not. You start down, only you're really going up; you are going left, only your needle indicates right. Blink your eyes. Trust your instruments. You learn the unqualified meaning of the word *trust*. Trust the Vibrator.

The instructors were very, very leery of night flying, especially with their first nest of gal pilots. My instructor was more than nervous. He was paranoid. "OK..." he stretched a gasp of relief inside the word, "let's descend," and I could hear

----

*Those crude prototypes can hardly qualify as forerunners of the hi-tech fighter planes to come 40-50 years later. Once the sound barrier was shattered with the advent of the jet, human muscle was replace with hydraulic power (somewhat in the way power steering transformed car driving). One light fingertip turns these harnessed rockets---lay a heavy finger on one and you barrel-rolling umpteen times. To come was the Stealth Bomber with its radar cover, and the sleek F-l6 family that can fly ground-to-target all on computerized navigation. It can drop bombs with pinpoint accuracy from 30,000 feet. The Mach 2, at 40,000 feet, can compute at l,320 mph.

In my time the pilot flew the plane. Today the plane flies the pilot. Mainly what he does is what the contemporary sports car driver does: sit in his computer-on-wheels and hope all systems and their backups remain in order.

him utter under his breath, "Thank God for little green apples." That seemed to be his prayer. It made me sore. I pulled the throttle back to its limits and nosed down---he grabbed the throttle and pushed it forward with great vigor. "Don't you ever do that again!" he yelled ominously. "You wanta yank the engine out of this thing---Don't answer, just head back to the field---Can you manage that much?"

Night landings were another misadventure. The lighting in those days, both on the airport and in the aircraft, was, by modern standards, designed for suicide. It was hard to tell when we were actually landing. No matter which one was supposed to be landing it seemed we were both on the stick fighting each other. "Don't-level-off-yet!" he ran the words together. "I might touch down if you'd get your hands off!" I fairly screamed. If in the next split second we didn't go cart wheeling into eternity, I was doomed anyway. I had committed the unpardonable. You don't rail back at flight instructors in tight situations.

"I'm recommending another instructor for you," he said cryptically as his soles touched solid ground. "We've got a personality problem, to put it civilly."

But he was the best instructor by far. "I want to stay with you!"

It stopped him in his tracks. "Pl-ease!"

I had flattered old Gruff-Tuff.

From then when he soloed me for night work, I got to work it all by myself, While he sat in the flight lounge drinking coffee. From this experience I learned in my many years of instructing, even today with my young granddaughters, never to grab or put my hands on the yoke with a student until death is absitively and posilutely certain.

Chapter 5

THE MIGHTY NORTH AMERICAN

I STILL think my favorite of all airplanes, until I got to pursuits, was the advanced trainer, the T6. It was a joy to fly. With 650 horses out there you could really eat up that Texas sagebrush l5 feet above ground.

Also we got training in advanced aerobatics, the slow rolls, the immelmans, spins and so on. It took me back to my introduction to flying in Cleveland with Smiling Joe. We roared over the field, peeled off, and circled to a beautiful three-point landing. Life was full and running over.

Maybe I have a special spot in my heart for this plane, because in later life I was to own one and get many laurels on pylon racing in the Cleveland National Air Races.

Instrument flying was much easier in the advanced trainer, even under the same hooded canopy, and at a faster airspeed. One reason was because I now had a calm Texas-bred trainer. Pinkie, unlike Gruff-Tuff, never yelled, never got upset, in fact never hurried. He was the slowest mortal I ever saw involved in this lightning-fast business. But he was epitome of smoothness.

The final part of advanced training brought us to the altar of the Bamboo Bomber. If a 747 had been rolling in those days, I don't think us could have been more impressed. Two engines--- What a monster! We clambered over it. We would go up in groups in the UC 78, and swap seats. That way we got to see each other's goofs. Besides, we got to be in the air more. That's what training was all about.

Throughout all our training we had half flight time and half ground time. Some groups had ground school in the AM, and flight time in the PM, and vice versa. Many an hour we sat learning Morse code, all types of navigation including celestial, aircraft and engines, meteorology , and on and on. It was a thrill, all of it. From early morning roust out to night taps, my cup ran over. The calisthenics, the running, the marching... we became very adept at it all, and put on special programs for visiting generals. At first there was a contest between the cadets and cadettes. But Sweetwater soon shipped the cadets out to other bases. It made things easier on the den mothers.

When we had our evening confabs about what we hoped to do when we graduated, Thumper and I wanted to ferry pursuit planes. We heard the gals in some of the ferry groups were already doing that. I didn't know if my heart could stand the thrill, even if my legs could somehow stretch to reach the rudder.

It never occured to me, in my callow self-centeredness, that if there had been no war there would have been no *WASP*s. No glory. It might be costing Holocausts and millions of lives, and my Swede might be over there dropping bombs on civilian populations. If there was one place on earth I'd rather have been, it would be there beside him as his copilot. Talk about glory! Superpowers might launch arms races for 40 years after the war, into the Nuclear Age, bankrupting the world. But at the time, would I have had it any other way? What mortals on this planet could be thinking any other way at the time? There were some. I didn't know them then.

The big anxiety clawing at the livers of Thumper and me was the words of our godmother, Jacqueline Cochran: 'Instructors only; too short to reach rudders'. We managed when we had a physical, to put bandaids under our heels and sometimes even to get away with cotton balls. We practiced standing tipped forward a bit on the balls of our feet until we could do it easily and without detection. Sometimes we managed to stretch half an inch. Our height charts looked like barometers. Many a nurse scratched her head.

The nine months at Sweetwater were as if they had wings to match the planes and our hearts. For most of us it was the most exhilirating time of our lives. The only time we left the town was during short intermissions between primary, basic and advanced training.

One of our group interludes was a trip to Carlsbad. Everybody talked about going to New Mexico because it was not a dry state. You could actually go to a bar and order a drink. Most of us were not indulgers, so to speak. For me, it was a blast to go into the Sweetwater drug store, order a coke and slip a little still-brew in it, under the table. What hurt was the restriction.

Off we went to Carlsbad, to explore the Caverans and visit a bar. We managed to put enough alcohol in our blood to keep from freezing down in the deep. Not having imbibed in a month of Sundays, we were a bit tipsy. The guide announced that the elevator was leaving near the end of the trip to take the elderly and infirm, and evidently we qualified, as he saw to it that we were first to go up.

As much as we would have liked to put it off, graduation day came. We were thrilled with our new assignment. Thumper and I got what our hearts were set on, the Ferry Command. We jumped up and down till we compacted the inch we had forged. There was one disappointment. Thumper was assigned to the ferry base at Romulus MI. I was assigned to the Fifth Ferry Division at Love Field, Dallas TX. I couln't wait to call Swede. His news was not so happy. There was talk of shipping troops overseas.

NICKIE & T6

T6 NORTH AMERICAN

UC 78 TWIN
(BAMBOO BOMBER)

Chapter 6

DAUGHTERS OF FIFINELLA

WHAT a happy day, arriving at Love Field, Dallas. All of us assignees from Sweetwater were driven from the railroad station in a staff car. The city of Dallas was neat and clean, and, of course, some city compared to Sweetwater. What made Dallas more exciting was the many P5l's ferried out there at Love Field.

We fell in love with Dallas in the first ten minutes. The clean buildings, the big green lawns and neat houses. We fell in love, all over again on a magnified scale, with the big plains, the clean air, well, Texas. The Base was neat too. Everything was fresh. It was spring. And I was in love, more than all else, with flying.

We got our BQ (Bachelor quarters) assignments. We were shown the officers' club, the rec hall, and all the facilities. Then that beautiful flight line, the twin Beeches, the A26's and on and on.

At the end of the first day we all went over to the officers' club and ordered steaks, while the rest of the country counted ration coupons.

The big thrill was watching the board for our first ferry assignment. That, of course, would not come until after a rehearsal in all the training basics, starting with the trainers, the PT and AT (Preliminary, Basic and Advanced Training routines).

Then---there it was posted: NICKIE CARTER. a BT to Macon GA. Winning the sweepstakes could not have thrilled me more. I got my B-4 bag packed and ready to go at six AM next morning.

That night the phone rang. My Djgooblie Swede was calling from Alabama. He had graduated that day. "Not much time for a honeymoon," he said, "but I've got the ring and I'm on my way!"

"You kidding?" I went in to shock.

He was at the station, ready to board the train to Dallas to marry me! Oh Lord what had I done? The dust storm of Sweetwater country must have clogged my senses. It was sweet to be engaged and have something to talk to the gals about. But really? Here I was in Dallas surrounded by all these gorgeous officers who were thrilled to pieces to entertain *WASP*s, and ferrying planes with them, and RONing (Remaining Over Night) with them at the night bases.

There was no stopping Swede. His ticket was bought. He was on his way.

"But I'm leaving on my first ferry flight---To Georgia---I'll fly right over the train you're on!"

"I'll wait for you in Dallas, my ferry princess. I've got a whole week. I'm not going overseas till you're my wife."

No putting this out of my life. Not unless, maybe, we got weathered in for two weeks in Macon. Maybe by then Swede would be gone overseas and ... who knows?

Four of us took off next morning with four BT's to deliver. A real assignment! No playing cross-country games. We took turns leading the legs on the flight, and had an uneventful trip to Macon. Nothing to romanticize for future generations. We stayed in a typical Georgia hotel, that is, we celebrated southern style on mint juleps. We celebrated my upcoming wedding with all kinds of conversation and speculation, none of it helpful. I would be tied down to this one guy for life. Yes, but he was headed overseas. Maybe he wouldn't make it back and you'd get his Air Force insurance policy---practical, coldhearted speculations by warmhearted friends. "Whatever you do, don't get pregnant."

We were all in a dither to check the weather. Charlotte got the report. She beamed at me. "You're in luck, Dum Dum." Then her words ran together in a streak. "Warm front moving in---No chance of getting out---May last days!"

Swede was pacing up and down in Dallas, with all arrangements made. I was stuck in Macon, sipping mint juleps. The warm front passed in two days. On the fourth day we were winging back to Dallas in a T-6, a plane we had to pick up and return.

On Saturday during a downpour, with the taxi waiting, meter running, there was performed one of the most unromantic, abbreviated ceremonies on record before a justice of the peace. Then the short-short honeymoon and my husband was on his way to New York for shipment overseas on Monday. He called from New York minutes before embarking, headed for the European theater of war.

His last words were, "I have something to fight for now."
Bye, dear Swede.

IT is not my intent to bemean the sacredness of human commitment and the marriage pact. I am simply recalling the way I found myself treating it in my callow girlhood. My relationship with Swede was too fractionated, too skimpy to be profound. For my part at least. It was not the course deep abiding love should take. And it was hardly a foundation for what was to come.

Other war brides were sitting home, grieving and praying for a loved one they might never see again. My first love was simply not, never had been, their kind of love. Total commitment, man to woman, woman to man. That was theirs.
It was Swede's. Marriage and family and all that goes with it. Family as a divine institution that forms the basic unit of society. It was all that to Swede: God's purpose for man and woman to become one, multiply, fill the earth. All that.

I guess if I had thought it out in concrete terms I would have reasoned that the human family had somehow missed the mark, what with a world full of fools blowing each other apart as if to depopulate the planet, now that it was filled like a cesspool and going wild and paranoid over sex and greed and lust for power and kingdoms. If God wanted the earth filled and subdued why couldn't he clean out of it all polluters, resurrect enough deserving ones out of all the billions that have come and gone, and fill the earth with decency?

From 16 to 20 I had one thing foremost in mind and that was wings. Swede, wonderful person that he was, had come into my life to share a dream. Only, as we were to learn, our dreams were horizons apart. My heart still flew the literal skies on

27

sheetmetal and canvas wings. My most exciting heartthrobs came from my most memorable flights. Anyone, for instance, seeing us in flight in open cockpits in wintertime would have thought they were being invaded by Martians. The garb we wore would have smothered an Eskimo. Fur lined pants, fur lined jackets,fur lined helmets, goggles, chamois skin face masks with eye and ear holes only . We wore gloves over mittens. When we walked our legs straddled three feet apart. I doted on things like that more than a kiss from my beloved stolen in a movie theater.

We ferried transports across country 300 miles at a hop, like grasshoppers. But it was fun. It took a lot of bourbon to thaw out the arteries during the evening RON.

On the leg from Phoenix to Palm Springs the crew leader said, "OK, gals, my boyfriend is based at Blythe. When we get there we're gonna descend and circle and give them one whale of a buzz job. I just called him on the phone. They'll be waiting."

After that we'd land at Palm Springs. She even had planned for the weather to move in and hole us several days in Palm springs.

Off we went and there was Blythe, and we gave it everything Evelyn asked for. My buddy Gayle and I got carried away. When we look up, after the buzzing, the four other planes were nowhere in sight. They had gone.

There was no way, at l,000 feet, to get our flight charts out of the baggage compartment. All we had to go on was my memory. I remembered that Palm Springs lay at the foot of some high mountain. Gayle showed utter confidence in me. She tucked her wing in close to mine and signaled me on.

I struck out in a westerly direction. We went through valleys and over mountains. Palm Springs was not appearing on our route. But what appeared on the ground was something that looked like a bomb target. We were over a bombardier target area. I tucked tail for a railroad and followed that. A railroad always heads for town---some town. But how far?

Our tanks were getting close to Empty. Ahead the sky was getting swallowed up darkly, not by night but that storm Evelyn predicted, coming in from the Pacific Coast.

At some point well beyond exasperation an airport did appear. We circled, looking it over, while in my mind I was preparing my little speech. By the time we hit the ramp I felt pretty sure I could find out where we were without letting anyone know we were lost.

But Gayle nudged into the pattern and taxied up ahead. When I wound down my engine she was standing on the wing, a straddle-legged Fifinella in her fur regalia, announcing, "So this is Palm Springs!"

"It's Victorville, lady!"

Gayle turned to me and folded. "Oh God, Nickie!"

It was too late to go up against that storm. We weathered it, four days, in Victorville.

When we got back to headquarters in Dallas, we were assigned an extra month in the PT's for straying from the group. To this day when I fly over Blythe I think of Evelyn and get indigestion.

My Dallas love, flying,was going beautifully. I ferried tons of T6 North Americans, and C47s and and DC3s , to mention a few. Our crew ferried the new Beeches , now known as the Dl8. When any of us buzzed our home town we felt like a queen, and we'd land at the local airport to show it off to our families. Clyde OH was buzzed so many times I wondered how the water tower survived.

Pittsburgh was a favorite stop. There we could count on the weather to be sour. The black smoke invariably would keep visibility down for days. We got so busy partying that once in awhile someone would forget to check the weather. It was a shock each time to find the black smoke had departed for Harrisburg and everyone was gone but you.

In the summertime flying planes, especially a BT or T6 with the greenhouse top, over Arizona or Texas, was a girl's favorite sport. Many a *WASP* got a full topless suntan. At 8,000 feet over Texas where could you find a more private spa? Still, you had to watch out for the unexpected. Once I was working on a competitive suntan, relaxing that hot afternoon in the cockpit privacy of a T6, headed for Big Springs. I had the greenhouse

29

cracked a couple inches for ventilation. It was time to start my letdown. I nosed it over and as I reached for my bra and blouse, the suction beat me to the grab. Out went my top clothing over the plains of Texas. What a jamb! One thought was to land, pull the cord on my parachute and wrap up. But how could you explain it? That would bring down all the restrictions in the book. The safest thing to do was to backtrack to Sweetwater and call the den mother to meet me at the end of the runway.

So far as I know it was a *WASP* first. Years later when the Fifinellas, the organization of the *WASP*s, held a reunion with Bob Cummings as MC, they staged a Texas farmer coming forward with a tattered bra and blouse in his hand to return to the owner. No other Daughter of Fifinella claimed it. I, for one, remained quiet.

At Brownsville TX we underwent pursuit training. This was the epitome of flying. Among the big fighter planes the P5l is still the king of reciprocating engines for the sports flyer.

Our training in flying fighter aircraft was until then confined to struggling in the back seat of the T6. They got us proficient in that, then they stuck us in the fighters and prayed a lot. I was having a blast. But then my pudgy instructor tried to date me. I remembered something as out of the past, that I was married. My husband was in England flying bombing missions over Germany. I gave Pudgy the icy shoulder without being polite. That was a mistake. He got my grade slips and downgraded me. I was sent back for more T6 training. It made me furious. I reported it to my guardian angel Cochran. She came burning the wind in her Air Force transport. There was a steamy investigation. Fatso was sent overseas to fly the Hump of China.

ALL this was kindergarten games compared to the jolt I got the morning I was jarred out of bunk to face a commission of high and mighties from Washington D.C. It had to do with some correspondence with my husband. It seemed strange to hear these Federal investigators call Swede "Your husband, Mrs. Johnson". I had lived with my husband Mr. Johnson one short day. Besides, I had not heard from him in weeks. Before that there had been a letter from faithful Swede almost every day. I had tried to find out what had happened to him. I had fired off a cablegram to his outfit in England, wording it subtly, referring to his aircraft, "How's Mr. D coming along?" It was the subtlety that brought the security VIPs soaring down from the Capitol. The conundrum had to do somehow with Mr. D. "Who is Mr. D?"

I tried to explain about *Djigooblie*. That made things vastly worse. I went over and over the reasoning and the message and the wording. They went over and over it, X-raying ever letter in every word for some code to pick up on. I understood. Swede would understand. But not them.

They came back. "Would you please, Mrs. Johnson, explain once more?" Once more, twice more, three times I explained about *Djigooblie*. It was Swede's plane. "We can't seem to get it down," they apologized in a suspicious tone. "We have to go back and explain this to the President."

Oh Lord, would the President try to explain it to Jacqueline Cochran? What they could not explain to me was that the Allied Command's plan was coming up for D-Day. It appeared that maybe Swede and I knew something about D-Day that they didn't know.

AFTER Brownsville it was back to Dallas and more of ferrying those magnificent pursuit craft around the country. What a grand and glorious holiday we gals were having, a holiday of sharing in squandering the country's resources on wings made for war. The buzz-overs over our home town were nearly indescribable in the local newspaper. We were the glory gals. We had reached the pinnacle.

Then came the Big News. The end of the war in the European theater. The Daughters of Fifinella had just about reached the point we never dreamed could come. It couldn't be, but it was: Our mission was winding down. It was like going into mourning. Our glamor world was fading.

As the boys started coming home we got mopup assignments, inglorious in their very nature. I was shuffled off to Eagle Pass TX to tow targets. We began to gripe in military fashion.

I know in my own case I was too young and too infatuated with flying to have my head on straight. As for the way the *WASPs* were dismissed, I, for the most part, echoed the complaints of the more seasoned pilots. As I mentioned earlier, we were not exactly military. The Air Force never issued us anything more dignified that male flight coveralls. Yet we were from day one under strict military discipline. Oh sure, male politicians had promised us all the benefits and status the military afforded. But when it came to a vote, after more than a year the men in Congress knuckled under a lobby of 10,000 well paid male civilian instructors who feared that with the War closing down they might lose some of their precious jobs to us. At most the *WASPs* numbered 1,830. Of these, 1,074 graduated. Thirty-eight lost their lives. We flew 12,650 planes of 77 different types. We ferried more than half the highspeed planes in the United States war effort. We logged about 60 million miles. We engaged in World War II up to our hairdos, deserving our share of the glory or guilt or whatever there was to go around. One male writer, H.R. Kaplan, may not have liked what we did to the pride and security of his gender, but he did find a kind word for us: "They had shattered many closely held male taboos about the physical and emotional capabilities of women to function effectively under stress and the sexual landscape would never be the same again. They were, in fact, among the earliest pioneers in the ongoing struggle to broaden female opportunities in a male-dominated world."

Speaking of uniforms, in the spring of 1944 Jackie Cochran at her expense outfitted us in blue slacks, battlejacketsand berets.

AND speaking of the transfer to Eagle Pass, that was indeed one of the crumb jobs still open to some of us, one of the dregs at the bottom of a bitter cup. It was the most dangerous assignment in all my *WASP* experience.

First, you were trained in how to tow a target. This training involved the use of radio control. You didn't control yourself. You were strapped into a tiny PQ8 craft. The idea was to see if another pilot in a "mother ship" could control you, from take-off to landing, by radio. If you've seen a kid from age 6 to 60 manuevering a toy race car in and out of some cul-de-sac, well just transfer that to a plane at l0,000 feet and you in it, zooming and diving and cavorting at the whim of a pilot in another plane.

Now this was mere training, mind you, in preparation for the real mission. That was to tow targets. Targets for live ammunition practice. Live targets we gals called them. Because the ones taking the target practice were the ones manipulating your plane however they pleased, shooting at the target, a sleeve-shaped muslin sack you were dragging behind you. You're flying through miles of flak and watching 90-millimeter shells burst around you---Who'd want to be closer to the front lines than this? Hey, guys, how about swapping roles? If females don't have the moxie for frontline duty, what are we doing here?   More than once I'd return with holes in the tail section.

To make matters more gross, the planes they gave us had seen their days. They were old, war-weary and mechanically unreliable. None of us will ever blot out of our minds what happened to *WASP* Mabel Rawlinson. She was checking out an A24 when the plane actually broke up in the air, burst into flames and smashed into a swamp. Before they could rescue Mabel the flames ate her alive.

When they got through using us for target practice, we held a wake over the whole affair at Eagle Pass. Then we all went over to Matamoras, Mexico, to drown our sorrows in a final margarita.   The girls then scattered into oblivion.

Were we the only self-centered souls to go into mourning because World War II was over? Or maybe it's not fair to put it that way. I was glad the war was over. I can't say my conscience was ever at ease over the fact that had there been no war there would have been no *WASP*s. If it had been some other way, I would have made it in aviation or died trying. So would some other gals. Maybe we wern't simply coldhearted opportunitists.

What came to bother me, as it did Swede when he was over there in it, was that we joined with our country the same as did people in enemy countries, feeling as they did that our side was unquestionably right, blessed by the clergy if not by God. Meanwhile you benefit personally in the process, if you look at

33

things short range. In this case, the process, a mighty nation at war, uses you and spits you out, and then you feel injured. Still waving your flag, because you came out victorious, but you still feel hurt and abused. You stand for a system that is the limit of your horizon. What would you do if the system went down and you had no horizon beyond that?

Anyway, by the time the Eagle Pass assignment was over, fractious Nickie Carter, alias Twitter, had undergone a lot of seasoning and had learned a lot of military gripese. After all, we were summarily dismissed, fired, to use the proper word, with hardly a "Kiss my grits". The glory days were forever gone. The hometown press hardly noticed when we came home. What we brought back was a $70,000 education in aviation with nowhere in the civilian world to put it to use. Congress had betrayed us. Veterans could look for a pension and VA benefits. We could look to tattered memories.

What happened to the ex-*WASP*s? It can be a blessing not to know the future. It would be 34 years, yes not till 1977, before Congress passed legislation recognizing us as veterans, pilots who had done dangerous duty when their country needed them. The law gave us retroactive eligibility for veteran's benefits. Two years after that, well hallelulia! the Air Force adopted us as part of its own.

I got a letter from my Swede at last. He had finished his 50 missions. He was being assigned to the United States. He was coming home.

This should have compensated for just about anything. But why did I have a leaden heart? My real feeling was one I could not honorably and justly admit to my inner self. But it was there, unspoken. If I could not have my first love, what need had I for the second?

SWEDE IN ENGLAND WITH HIS P51
DJIGOOBLIE

Chapter 7

FREEDOM, A STATE OF MIND

FREEDOM. Sometimes it is so precious. But, so it seemed, it was not for the famous Cochran gals. Our wings were clipped. We were cut off from what was precious to us---those beautiful airplanes, the freedom of flight. It was sudden shock. There were all kinds of reactions. Some of the gals married their old instructors. Some married lieutenants they ferried planes with. Some joined the Red Cross, the Nurse Corps, anything to have a final fling.

I looked at the letter I got from Swede. He was so elated to be coming home. Home to his wife, his family, to start a new life. He envisioned it as something beautiful and longed for, something to last a lifetime. This added to my problems and my decisions. Who needed a white fence and garden when you couldn't fly? I looked at my half-filled application for the Red Cross. I tore it up.

I followed Swede to where he was stationed in Alexandria LA. It did not help to have him going to the air base every morning while I trudged the streets for a job, something to do. Finally I went to the base and took a job in the sheet metal department. Dullsville. The foreman did not relish teaching a fledgling. I refused to work in the office. At least I wanted to touch a plane.

But it was not like Lock Haven. The thrill of the first flight hours was not there. The foreman did at last find a place for me. I was the only one who would fit in the fuselage of a P40 through the baggage door. My job was to crawl in and buck rivets for the installation of the relief tubes (the equivalent of plumbing pipes from the toilet). He put me there to get me out of sight. But I was touching an airplane, even though sprawled on my back in the dark, bucking rivets. A place to contemplate the joke I heard. This man was asked after spending twenty years cleaning johns why he did not get a more upgraded job and he said, " What? And leave aviation?"

Relief came when Swede got transferred to another base at Columbus GA. There I got a job at the local airport. Flying at last! I got my instructor's rating and began teaching. I loved it. It was not ferrying a P51 or an AT6, but how could I knock it? It was flying. It kept me out of the fuselage.

My students were for the most part paratroopers stationed at the local base. Most of them had many, many jumps but had never touched an instrument panel. They felt more comfortable bailing out at 3,000 feet.

The hours built up rapidly. On weekends I did not even leave the cockpit of the J3 cub or cut the engine between students. I was back in love again.

But this was at the same time the beginning of 30 years of marital troubles that were never eased. Aviation incompatibility, you might call it. Swede was left at home evenings and weekends. Being conventional and Swedish (I don't say that in a disparaging way), he was stuck with the old-fashioned idea that a wife's place is in the home serving dinner at 5:30. I was just not programmed for that. I had, in fact, warned him of that before our marital contract. My feeling toward flying was not shared, as I had thought it was. What he had been carried away by was the idea of the Air Force, the cadets, the uniforms, and fighting the Big War. But routine flying in the civilian world? For Swede? No. Fifty bombing missions over Germany was all the flying he ever wanted to do.

I was not the only gal who ended up married to a burnout pilot. I got a letter from my *WASP* buddy Gayle. "Can you imagine?" she wrote, "This cadet I married from Sweetwater wants to settle down in Oklahoma and sell insurance!" In the next five years the divorce rate among *WASP*s probably outstripped the national average. Women's lib arrived in the flying world before most "liberated females" were born.

Swede was mustered out in Georgia. We started on a long auto trip to California. He decided if he wanted to save his marriage we would have to settle near an airport. By this time my dream was to own an airport in the Golden State.

We made the grand tour of Southern California. But like in gold rush days, somebody else had beaten me to it. We ended up back in Cleveland OH. I wasted no time getting to the Airport where Smiling Joe , my first instructor, had introduced me to the realms above. I had to settle for working part-time in the office and part-time instructing. Swede pursued his maintenance course, reasoning that if we were to have an airport in California (it was still my deathless determination to have it), someone would have to mend the planes. Working with his hands was his thing. The arrangement was a compromise. I wanted him to share flying as much as he wanted me to wear the apron. Neither of us ever got what we wanted.

One day this T6 landed and in came this tall giant with a hearing aid. The air races were pending in Cleveland. There were rumors about an all-girl's race with AT6's. I introduced myself to Captain Eddy. In the course of the chitchat I learned he had worked with radar during the War and was a television genius. With that behind us I got to what I was after: "I wonder if I could lease or borrow your T6 for the gal's race coming here?"

"Sure," he said, "No problem. Just call me and come out to Michigan City, Indiana, and pick it up."

Time sizzled. Plans materialized. The big air race was pending. And the Halle Trophy race was to be all women, limited to AT6 North Americans. I called Captain Eddy. "Come and get it," he said. I was off on the next train to Michigan City.

For two weeks I basked in the preparations for my first national air race. We polished that plane till it sparkled. It outshone the sun.

All the old air race pros were descending on Cleveland, landing their magnificent racers. Tony Levier, test pilot for Lockheed and pilot of a P38 in the race, rode with me to show me how to master turns around the pylons (the towers that marked the turns in the race). I met all the pros from the "Golden days of Air Racing", the days before the war. That was when they built their own planes---Ortman, Roscoe Turner and others. It was almost as exciting as being back in the *WASPs*.

The qualifying trials started. Days were filled with flying and practicing on the course, and nights with meeting the race crowd. "Swede even renewed his love of aviation" I soared in pure ecstasy. Then the big day came.

The Halle Trophy entries were lined up, eight of us gals. First there was the qualifying "race horse takeoff", a ground race long since abandoned. Swede taped me in the plane. I was literally sealed in. Every seam on the canopy was taped over. So were wing and fuselage seams. The engines were started and running. Flags changed close to the takeoff flag. Engines purred, louder and louder, and brakes held tighter and tighter. With all eight girls standing on the brakes and revving, the final flag dropped and off we shot, all heading for the first pylon. I can see why this phase was abandoned---a ground race with airplanes is utterly suicidal. Anyway the planes are lined up in the air nowadays by a lead plane.

Weight was a big factor in the race. We carried just enough gasoline to complete the rounds and land. This called for meticulous calculation. How embarrassing to be leading down the finish line and have the engine conk. Weight also called for balance. Half the gas in the left tank, half in the right. And you'd better not forget to switch tanks in the middle of the race. More than one pilot in those days landed kerplunk because of forgetting to count the laps. I stuck five tabs on my instrument panel, and each lap of the course I plucked one off. The red tab meant *Switch Tanks!*

This was a closed course race, 5 laps of a 15-mile course. The whole event was over in about 20 minutes. All that to climax a year's planning, weeks of trial runs, up all night with modification mechanics, oodles of expense and publicity for the sponsor, mountains of joy, canyons of heartaches, all crashing to a climax in 20 minutes. After that, pilots and fans falling all over you, parties and trophy conventions with you marching midst applause... or despair parties at the local snakepit with your crew, all lamenting and crying till your beer sloshed over, and courageous talk about next year....All this hanging over your head during those 20 glorious, excruciating minutes while you are trying to keep track of the other plane in close proximity and you are in an almost 90 degree bank rounding a pylon, flying a mere 75 feet above ground and doing an impossible but there it is--227 miles an hour in a lumbering T6.

In that first race I managed to take third place. It was immensely encouraging as we had only two weeks to prepare. But plans for next year! Hey I couldn't wait. Captain Eddy was elated. Immediately he started radio and television interviews. Being Mr. Television, it was easy.

I appeared on the Breakfast Club with Don McNeil, and all the shows around Chicago.   And the biggest news, so far as I was concerned, was that I had become, with my prize money, an interest, in fact a partner, in the T6 with Captain Eddy and our plans for the following year.

Chapter 8

A SEARCH FOR ROOTS

SWEDE and I went back to California, this time to take roots. With us came Rita and Harry, a couple from the Cleveland Airport. They had fallen in love and decided to get married. This trip with us, a three months excursion, was their honeymoon. We shared a fold-out camper hitched to the rear of our car. The trip out was really exploratory, as we stopped at every bend and zigged to south and zagged to north almost as much as we moved west. It reminded me of some of the old steersman courses in the ferry command.

Between the card games, explorations and sightseeing we finally reached California. Most of what we saw, in searching for that dream airport, was disappointing. Airports back east were green and neat and clean. When we poked around Gardena and Inglewood and Compton we were not bowled over by mud and Quonset huts. We lurked along the border at San Diego, basking in the sunshine and exploring airports. We might have been naive in thinking all we had to do was pick our airport and settle down. Most of what we found were owned by the Government and we were not enchanted by the looks of them. When I think that we tromped over the "mines field", now Los Angeles International (LAX), and could have had it with some red tape, I almost get ill thinking how dumb I was.

Rita became pregnant regardless of the crowded honeymoon quarters and we each got our own trailer. After we split up she became lonesome. Eventually they went back to Cleveland to settle down.

After bypassing all Government owned opportunities on airstrips, Swede and I chose to go into business at a little airport toward the desert called Claremont. Swede opened a maintenance shop. I became an instructor at the existing school.

We brought Captain Eddy's T6 out for race preparation. With the help of an ex-mechanic from North American, Swede tuned it up with a geared engine and groomed it down to the last detail. Excitement ran high at Cable Claremont. Finally we took off for Cleveland. We carried with us a prop ring to be installed to give that big engine and the three-blade prop the best race pitch.

That accessory was to cause some excitement during takeoff tryouts. The prop sometimes wanted to stay in high or cruise pitch and sometimes it took a couple of trials down the runway to coax it into low pitch.

The gals gathering at Cleveland had gotten into the swing of the race. There appeared all kinds of beautiful planes, highly shined, spectacular paint jobs, geared engines---inline ranger engines---the competition this year was going to be fantastic. The incline engine was sleek and took the qualifying trials over us by 10 miles an hour. We had to do something.

And we did. On the night before the race we tore off the canopy, rounded up a couple of welders who probably never saw an aircraft before, and with an old fuselage from an air coupe we sculptured our plane into a one-place cockpit, and faired the remainder sleekly downhill to the tail. Rivets were flying and torches were flaring. News reporters, who knew about as much about racer planes as they did midwifing, discounted us for even entering.

We worked all night to get ready for the race---barely in time. There I was, somehow in the line- up for the race horse takeoff to the first pylon.

The all-night hours paid off. I won first prize. I was national women's flying champion, an honor her Royal Highness Jacqueline Cochran would be proud of. What an exaltation it was to be guided to the winner's stand to receive my trophy, along with Paul Mantz and an Air Force winner.

My partner Captain Eddy was elated. Television cameras blazed. Radio stations crackled. We had made it to the summit in air racing. Even Swede grinned with pride. I got to experience the speeches and the trophy parties and all the fanfare of triumph, newspaper interviews and the elation of success. New horizons after all!

41

After a few weeks we returned, Swede and I, with our proud bird to California. The trip back posed a problem. We now had a one-place cockpit. We had to take turns riding in the fuselage, lying down with the parachute for a pillow. It meant total reliance on whichever one was in the pilot's seat. I mean that's total reliance. On my turns to be penned in the fuselage, I contemplated my chances of opening the baggage door and strapping on my parachute in time to pull the cord. It was an aerobatic feat which, so far as I knew, had never been done or never would be. It gave us something to think about during three-hour stints.

While I was piloting one leg the engine became exceedingly rough. I passed a note to my mechanic through a one-inch opening. He scribbled a reply on the back, "Try the carburetor heat." I tried. I tried everything. The engine kept getting rougher. It was going to be a test like I'd never been up against before. If the engine quit should I jump or try to make a crash landing? You are torn between affection and loyalty and self-preservation. That gets down to bedrock. Fortunately I was able to land the craft at Winslow AZ. Poor Swede crawled out of the hold wilted, shaky, grateful and more than ready to remedy the problem.

Finally the trip was over. We had a whole year to recover. The following year Swede decided to drive his car out ahead of time so we would have transportation in Cleveland. I got to fly the plane all the way both ways.

There was a new mix of emotions this time. As I was the previous winner I got a special dose of fanfare. Secretly I hoped those excruciating turns would not injure my daughter. I decided it would be a girl. She would take up Mama's wings in the world of flying.

By the fourth lap I was in the lead. Then an oil line blew. The cockpit filled with smoke. That's the way it goes in the world of air racing. That year, no fanfare. Just poor-me parties and too-bads from your colleagues.

My son was born a few months later. This helped distract me from the disappointments.

CAARTER READYING FOR NATIONAL CHAMPIONSHIP RACE.

NICKIE'S PLANE, "FASTEST IN THE AIR"
WINNING HALLE TROPY RACE.

CHAMPION BEING STOWED IN BAGGAGE
HOLD FOR RETURN FLIGHT TO CALIFORNIA.
HUSBAND SWEDE PREPARED FOR TAKE OFF.

One more trip to Cleveland a year later. And total disappointment. When they learned I had a son five months old they ruled me out of the race. Swede was pleased. I was bitter.

That year a P51 crashed into a home and killed a family. That did it. The last of the races. Beer flowed in the snakepits. Pilots moaned. The end of an era.

Chapter 9

WEDDED STRANGERS

STARTING with Cable Claremont I worked numerous airports up and down the Southern California Valley. Swede and I traveled from San Diego's Gillespie Field up the coast to Minesfield, now Los Angeles International (oh, if I had the sense to choose a leasehold here). We ended out at the foot of Baldy for the esthetic scenery.

It was during this period that, for the first time, Swede and I began to recognize each other, with all the surface niceties wearing thin, like old paint peeling off. We were holding each other at arm's length, so to speak, taking a wary look at each other, eye to eye.

Here we were, two kids meeting in the military, infatuated by the glamour of uniforms, starting wedded life with a one day honeymoon in a motel room, then good-by for years. I say "kids" because you wouldn't say we were adults in maturity and experience, would you? What a horrendous number of marriages are started off as frivolously as that! Hearts on fire with energies whipped alive by war. Kids, yes. When war comes don't we all refer to the ones doing the fighting as "our boys"? And how many of those eighteen-year-olds are not boys? Swede would sometimes burst out bitterly with things like, "There's sure as thunder one way to put a stop to wars. Pass a law that no man under 40 can be drafted. And make them that start the wars be the first to fill the trenches."

I was still too overturned by the way we gals were dumped out of the *WASPs* to pay much heed to Swede's attitude. Anyway, differences stood out like thorns piercing each other. Swede was a man free from obsessions. I was a woman consumed by one. Swede wanted to settle down to a steady job and routine family life. No force on earth could deter me from my fixed goal.

One thing that strained our bond was Swede's growing aversion to flying. I know it was my attitude that seeded that aversion and made it grow. I would try to make him see it my way. "You mean you don't just love to get in an airplane and fly and soar between the clouds, or buzz across the hills and desert? Don't you want to climb up and level out and relax, and look still higher and thank God and appreciate life, and look down and feel you've left behind and below all the silly cares of everyday life?"

He'd retort, "I've heard drug addicts talk about getting higher than that without lifting a foot off the ground." Then he'd go on about how the sight of an airplane took him back to combat missions. You're having your final cigarette before the crew chief signals the engine start, then off you go over Germany, looking for the enemy to appear to attack the B17 bombers you're covering. "Maybe if you girls in the *WASP* had shared combat flying it might dawn on you that a war was for some other reason than fame and glory."

It hurt. But on he'd go: "Then enemy planes appear, and what goes on is not for thrills, but to see who kills or gets killed. You talk about cavorting in the sky," he'd say, "You're trying to get behind or above the enemy, and you're watching a fellow plane, the Joe you sat with at the bar last night, talking about this whole fiasco called war. You glimpse him going down in flames . I tell you it has to do with heartstrings all right, the curse of flying and desecrating God's heavens."

Once started, Swede had to let it all out. "Finally you get back, many times limping with a shot-up plane that barely makes it. The crew chief meets you with a slug of whiskey, thanking God his own plane made it. And back to the bar...who'll be next? The Joe that didn't make it left you something, a share of his clothing. This nightly hand-me-down did things to your morale---at least to mine. Items keep changing hands day by day. Tomorrow who'll be next?"

Swede was never a fighter at heart. Like many guys he went to war in the most romantic fashion, the Air Force, all garbed out in resplendent uniforms, and the politicians and the preachers and the whole hullabaloo of the people cheering you on in God's name. "But when you get to thinking, that's exactly the euphoria that's propelling the guys at you from the other side. When I met an enemy face to face I bore no malice toward that Joe. It was either your life or his, and if he lost his, somehow yours didn't mean a lot to you any more."

One time, he said, he was flying a strafing mission, a ground shoot-up of railroad stations. He came down on a train close enough to see the engineer throw up his hands in a plea for mercy. "What'd I do? I didn't pull the trigger. I was not collecting medals and stripes like the aces. Let the heroes strut their medals."

All this could destroy a man's love for flying, I'd have to admit. I didn't want to see that the psychological impact might never be overcome. Maybe it shouldn't have been hard for me to understand, but it was. Maybe that was because I didn't want to understand.

Chapter 10

A KNOCK ON THE DOOR

SWEDE stuck with me longer than most men probably would have. It was torture for him as it was for me. But now we had a child to consider. We were a family, not too functional maybe, but a family

One main problem was to find some place to settle down and get stabilized. That was no problem for Swede. Almost anywhere there was an airport he could get a job in maintenance. The problem was me. It was not easy to find an airport needing a flight instructor. Swede had to pick up and follow me all the way up the Southern California coast. From San Diego's Gillispe Field up to Mines Field, now Los Angeles International, I searched. We ended out at the foot of Baldy for the esthetic scenery.

Scenery, however, was about all we had to brighten the days. Then, so far as my career in flying was concerned, there came what appeared to be the death blow. I was pregnant again. Would I ever go flying to the heights and chasing the clouds once more? It was that kind of down period when you wonder where this life is taking you.

Then came that Sunday morning and a knock on the door. I opened it and there stood a tall lady with a Bible in her hand .

"My name is Dorothy Zuck," she said in a quiet, friendly way. "This morning we are discussing with our neighbors the hope for a better world."

"We could use one," I said apathetically. I looked her up and down, wondering what would she know about a better world.

"Did you know that's what the Bible assures us of?"

I shrugged. It had something to do with the first three chapters of the Bible telling about Paradise lost, and the last three chapters telling about Paradise restored. All the three quarters of a million words in between had something to do with how what was lost is restored. And in the process Jehovah came out vindicated.

47

"For instance," Dorothy Zuck illustrated, "are you familiar with the Lord's Prayer?"

"Oh sure," I nodded. I had chanted it all my life like a tape recorder. "When I was a kid I didn't get the 'hallowed by thy name' part right. I thought it said 'hell by thy name'. I never understood why they called God 'Hell'"

She laughed almost to tears.

"Anyway," she said, "did you understand the part about God's will being done on earth as in heaven?"

If we understood what His will is, that should mean a better world, wouldn't it? And if we were to pray for it wouldn't our prayers be futile if there was not going to be a better world?

"Will there be airplanes?"

That almost threw her off track. I could see this was going to take some explaining. As I had opened the door with a question, I invited her in.

Dorothy Zuck hit the highlights from the first three chapters of Genesis to the last the chapters of Revelation. My mind was reeling.

"In order to fill your need I think you ought to have a home Bible study," she proposed.

It was too much to digest all at once. Here was someone outlining the Bible on a dime.

I was somehow disposed to learn more about it. Besides, Swede worked nights. Here was something that would help fill up those long evenings.

"Why not?" I said.

Dorothy suggested bringing her husband along. As she assured me later, this was the celebrated call of the day for that car group of Jehovah's Witnesses.

SO began a long and tedious trial for John and Dorothy Zuck. "Where does it say God's Name is Jehovah?" I challenged.

They had me read Psalms 83:18, King James Version: "Thou, whose name is JEHOVAH art the most high over all the earth."

I thought I knew enough to ask how they knew Jesus is not the New Testament name for Jehovah in the Old Testament. They showed me that Luke l: 32 in the New Testament presents Jesus as the "son of the Most High" of the Old Testament.

"Where," I challenged, "does the Bible say there is no Trinity?"

Where, they challenged, does it say there is one?

The preacher where I had gone to church once in a month of Sundays had prepared me with the King James Version of l John 5:7 which says the Father and the Word (Son) and the Holy Ghost are one. The Zucks showed me from revisions of the King James that the verse is a forgery.

But---"Doesn't the Bible say the earth is to be burned up?"

First, the Zucks asked me where hellfire is said to be located. I had heard some time or another that it is located in the bowels of the earth. They asked how long people are supposed to burn there.

"Forever."

"But", John pretended to be puzzled, "If hell is in the midst of the earth and the earth is burned up, how can hell last forever?"

Back and forth it went. Not an argument nor a conflict. But without realizing it I had accumulated a mass of religious thinking from my Sunday School background and from Swede' occasional ideas from his Lutheran teachings. Jehovah's Witnesses were going to prove that church teachings do not hold a single doctrine in accurate knowledge. In that situation I challenged every proof text over and over. It had to be set straight in my mind from every approach. Surely the Zucks never worked harder for a proselyte. But no convert comes easy. In l992 you could divide the one billion hours of evangelizing reported by the Witnesses by the third of a million converts baptized for the year and you come out with about 3,333 hours devoted to getting one person baptized.

Anyway John Zuck once told me a story to illustrate that although I might be sincere, I didn't catch on like lightning. A traveler with a radio approached a native in deepest Africa. "How come talk?" the native asked. The traveler explained in great

49

detail about electrical currents, the wiring, the circuitry, speakers and all that. Then he said, "You understand?" The native said, "How come talk?"

Before long I was going to their meetings, the special talks, even the assemblies. By now I was dragging my two-year-old and then the newborn baby, and the necessary entrapments. Dorothy and John had long since raised their one boy. They were being indoctrinated back into child raising. The patience, the long-suffering and endurance this couple had to put up with in trying to help me on the road to life is a lesson in Christian fortitude I have tried to model my own life after in my later years at least.

Swede, who had long ago learned not to stand in the way of my aberrations, tactfully did not try to dissuade me. But he himself would have nothing to do with it. I know he hoped it was all a stress reaction on my part that would go away.

Chapter 11

MIXED HORIZONS

DURING this interlude of spiritual awakening, I tried something I never thought possible for me. I choose to leave aviation for the more practical and lucrative field of advertising. This was after my second child was born. I could work only a few hours a day and have more time for my growing family. Like everything else I attempted, I poured my heart into advertising. "All that your hand finds to do, do with your very power," the Zucks taught me from Ecclesiastes 9:l0, "for there is no work nor devising nor knowledge nor wisdom in Sheol, the place to which you are going." Only the Zucks did not mean to go to extremes, especially in secular pursuits, because the Bible also teaches, "Let your reasonableness become known to all men."---Philippians 4:5.

I became western states representative for the firm, getting more and more involved and traveling so much that once again I was swallowed up full time. So my purpose was self-defeating.

I quit. Then I went to Ontario Airport, determined to instruct part time. That's where I met Bud Kagen. A meeting that led to my eventual downfall.

Not that I blame Bud. At that time Bud was feuding with the FAA (Federal Aviation Administration). Their offices were upstairs over Bud's. When I went to work for him they warned me that he was under their gun. I took the job anyway, since it was legitimate and the pay was good.

Bud not only dealt fairly with me. The main thing is, he gave me the opportunity to fly again. So far as the FAA was concerned, what right did they have to control another's lifestream?

Self-willed determination was not something I came by accidentally. My widowed Mom had that kind of grit in her genes. She taught us kids by word and deed the meaning of independence, My two brothers, Don and George Carter, and I grew up as they say in the Ozarks, "As independent as a hog on ice." George worked hard and after school went into the Army and from there into Maritime, where he has been all his life. Don stayed in the home town, got to be successful in real estate and eventually became mayor of Clyde. Clyde OH, by the way, was the "Peyton Place" of Sherwood Anderson's *Winesburg Ohio.*

(In case Sherwood Anderson and his book were before your time, *Winesburg*, which came out in 1919, was X-rated and banned from Clyde's library. Recently the Today Show on TV featured a revival of Anderson's novel. When everybody was tipped off that it was a naughty book there was a rush by the sensation-seeking generation of the '90s to read it. What a letdown! The most risqué chapter is about a high school teacher who had an apartment downtown from which he could watch a female disrobe in front of a drawn shade.)

Anyway, I was always the apple of my mother's eye, being a girl and so adventurous and, in her eye at least, a famous aviatrix. How she delighted in concocting stories about her daughter's conquests as National Air Race Champion and former *WASP*, for the Clyde *Enterprise.* Mom died in the hospital ten days after my arrest by Monda, and I never knew if the news reached her and broke her heart.

At Southwest Aviation in Ontario I derived an education in promoting a flight school from Bud Kagen. The relationship, sad to say , ended prematurely because Bud's feud with the FAA was headed in only one direction. It was his downfall.

MEANWHILE, my fixation on flying as the ultra achievement in life was colliding with a spiritual challenge. Is there really a grander horizon? People like the Zucks were telling me words to this effect: 'Your biography, past, present and future is set down in one verse in the Book of Life. Here it is, in the beginning chapter of the Bible, Genesis 1:26: "God said, 'Let us make man in our image, in our likeness." The next verse adds: "In God's image he created him; male and female he created them."

"What is your purpose for being here? To image your Creator. That is the long and short of it. That doesn't rule out flying as a profession. But then the profession comes second." So quoth the Zucks.

But how do you image Someone you can't see? Well you learn about his personality. Four cardinal personality traits stand out, exercised in perfect balance: Love, Wisdom, Justice and Power. You have to learn in accurate knowledge what they mean. Then you learn how to adapt them in your own personality. In the process your own personality traits, fashioned after this world's values and experience, are gradually sloughed off and replaced by the divine personality traits. Off with the old nature. On with the new. How hard, oh how hard when your old personality is glazed over with a stainless steel will.

Chapter 12

SWEDE'S HORIZON

MY life never before was pitched into such turmoil. For one thing there was the business. I was starting a new venture in developing my own flight school at Ontario. But, as mentioned, I was starting under a cloud. After Bud Kagen left , the FAA seemed never to forget how I ignored them. It seemed to me they took that as an insult. It didn't matter that I had tried to remain neutral and tend to my own business of teaching people to fly. Everything I pursued, now that I was on my own, if it required their certification, somehow it became harder for me than for competing operators. Finally, after qualifying several times over, I became an FAA examiner---I attribute it to my friend, chief of GADO (General Aviation District Office), who was retiring, and who granted my certification. "If I don't give it to you Nickie," he said, "you will never get it from these people."

Yet while I had it I was constantly under fire. At the drop of a hat the designation was removed. I would hire a lawyer and get it back. A few months later, gone again. I was scoring more losses than gains. I gave it up as a lost cause. "I think the Devil is after me," I told the Zucks.

"He's after everybody who tries to break loose from his system of things," they assured. The raw, vicious spirit of the business world brought out the worst in me, and overwhelmed the peace and harmony that were supposed to prevail at home and among my widening circle of spiritual brothers and sisters. "Continue putting up with one another and forgiving one another freely" was up against being all day long in an environment of "wrath, anger, badness, abusive speech" and mouths spilling over with obscene talk.

It was too much, this "Clothing yourself with love, the perfect bond of union", too much coming on too fast. Where the old personality showed up worst was where it should have showed up best, at home. I was not easy for a mild tempered man like Swede to put up with.

The cutting edge showed in bombarding my worldly friends and associates with my newfound religion. I threw Bible principles at them etched in stone, to cut down, not to build up. "Take drunkenness and gluttony and anxiety over gifts out of Christmas, and what's left?" "What do bunny eggs and spring finery have to do with the resurrection of Christ?"

Mildness and self-control would come gradually, as I approached dedication, the Zucks hoped. After many a frustrating session, John and Dorothy were nervously surprised when I appeared ready to leave for an assembly with my bathing suit for baptism.

UNDER constant fire from the FAA, I gave up my initial attempt to start a flying school. But not for long. I went across the hall to Ontario Flight Service to work for Jim Sconyers. What I didn't learn about promotion from Bud, I learned from Sconyers. He had the blessing of the FAA. To show you the irony of things, Jim and his partner Woody were novices, doing things horrendously wrong, getting by with potential murder. They had bought a couple of airplanes, learned to fly, leased the planes to a school. The school went under. The planes came back. My job: take over where the school left off.

I became their chief pilot. My biggest chore was to try to keep them out of trouble. There was nothing they would not dare. In their courses they neglected to read the Federal Air Regulations. You'd think they were pioneering the whole concept of aviation with the Wright brothers, writing the rules as they went along, teaching students to be aerial renegades. Without flight plans they'd fly in and out of Ontario International in all kinds of circumstances and conditions; they survived only by what was called Oakie's luck. Woody would fly across the whole country on instruments without proper ratings. To keep out of trouble he would just turn off his radios and proceed; Sconyers was a fitting pilot for him.

It was here during the mid-6's, the golden age for young guys to get on the airlines, that I taught students who became successful pilots. My favorite student was Tom Guthrie who went to TWA, along with Steve Holmes. A student named Nash went with Texas International. Fish McCloud went with PSA. Don Weldon never went with the airlines but worked with me at my various flight schools later on, until the end. When, in time, the FBI came down on me, Don and his wife Pixie remained my morale influence through it all.

At Ontario is where I met Carl Domschke , with Continental Airlines. We became friends and partners for many years in a Comanche airplane. That craft was my love of the single engine aircraft. It was to cause me much, much misery with the Federal bankruptcy court and Mr. Monda. Would that I had kept Carl Domschke as a partner instead of a double-crossing cheat who, among other things, accused me of stealing my own plane.

From Ontario I went to Chino, a move I always regretted, to try to establish my own flying school again. Roy Outson, chief of the Ontario GADO, granted me my flight examiner rating. I doubt if Roy had any idea of the battle it was going to be to hang on to that rating. My inspectors would always be tougher, my errors more glaring, my anger more intemperate. Other operators did the same things, made the same errors. They got by. I still lived under the shadow of Bud Kagen.

Meanwhile Swede had some health problems. Eventually he had to have a kidney removed. It was then we had him a captive audience. As he lay on the couch he could not avoid listening as John and Dorothy continued into their second year of attempting to 'set things straight' in my fired-up temperament. He compared his traditional Lutheran doctrines with what he heard us discussing from simple Bible statements, unglossed by theological attenuations, and perceived inconsistencies right and left. He was a much more apt a student than I. He was one of those persons Jesus must have had in mind when he said the sheep follow him, the fine shepherd, because they know his voice. He was one of those persons "rightly disposed" to become believers. The contrast between my husband and me was sharply drawn in time by a statement in *The Watchtower* when it said: "Some people, due perhaps to inheritance or environment, have more difficulty conforming to a Christian way of life than others do." That's me, I thought. Yet the next statement held out hope even for me: " But Jehovah assures us that anyone who is really willing to exert himself can do it."

Swede, to all our amazements, immediately grasped the truth he had avoided all this time. He was soon baptized. Before long we were engaged in all the activities, including door-to-door ministry ourselves and we opened our home to a Tuesday evening study for a small segment of the congregation, a segment with the potentiality of growing into a congregation on its own.

When wind and storm wear away the fascination that first attracted two persons to each other, which was flying, when one comes to abominate it, as Swede did flying, both are left with no solid attachments. Communication dries up. Mutual concern goes begging. Our spiritual union revived our relationship on a vastly elevated plateau as we realized no greater glory can be attained than to image our Creator. Still that did not bring halcyon peace and that oneness God spoke of when he married Adam and Eve. I was still, like Eve, a willful person, married to a plane more than to a man, not even the father of my children. Swede, maybe in conscious or subconscious self-defense, reacted by seeking his own diversion, or maybe I should say aberration. His was a classic car, a Kissel. .

I didn't like having to take the same medicine I was dosing out to him. We had many a disagreement over his obsession. Every weekend he spent working on that abominable relic.

"Why won't you let the kids play in the garage?"

"They might put a smudge on the new paint." Or, "They might start playing with some of those expensive parts."

"Why can't we go on a picnic with the Worth's at the park?"

"This is the Sunday I was going to prime the spare tire holder."

Evenings were long and lonely with Swede in the garage. Anyone who could become infatuated with a machine that couldn't fly was, in my opinion, off his duff. Every trip we took in the station wagon became related to a search for Kissel parts; and long hours were spent in junk yards, while he searched through piles of iron rubble and I tried to entertain two squirmy boys while restricting them to the station wagon or a bench in a dirty, smoky waiting room. To this day I detour salvage yards and will pay top dollar to Pep Boys for a part fresh from the factory.

This was the nature of our jousting before Swede began to outdistance me in displaying the "fruit of the spirit". But as we progressed spiritually Swede became an appointed overseer in the congregation. I grew more active in the ministry. The children responded to the prospects of seeing the earth rid of its polluters and the Paradise transformation to come. By the time Swede became Ministry School overseer, He sold the Kissel after seven years to a buyer who sold it to Harrah's Museum in Renoo, where it sits on display today. I could have learned something about divine wisdom, the kind that images the Creator, from his example. Wisdom is the use of knowledge. Swede had come to understand that. One of his favorite guidance texts came from the *New World Translation* of l Corinthians 6:l3: "All things are lawful for me; but not all things are advantageous. All things are lawful for me; but I will not let myself be brought under authority by anything." The way he liked to put it was: "No habit nor obsession is going to master me."

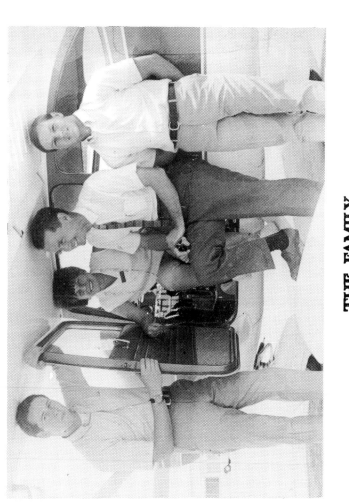

THE FAMILY
JOHN-NICKIE-SWEDE-SAM
CONVENTION AT DODGER STADIUM,1967

SWEDE AND THE KISSEL SPEEDSTER

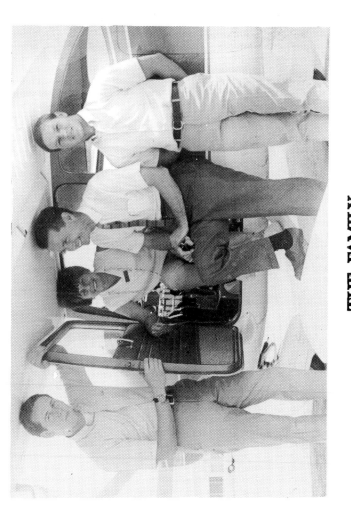

THE FAMILY
JOHN-NICKIE-SWEDE-SAM
CONVENTION AT DODGER STADIUM,1967

SWEDE AND THE KISSEL SPEEDSTER

Chapter 13

THE FLEDGLINGS

THE children progressed in the ministry as their age advanced. They were enrolled in the Ministry School at an early age. Our congregation was putting pizzazz into our Service Meeting demonstrations. We'd have productions to rival television dramas. World reports in the Theocratic News were dramatized in full dress regalia---if there was a peak of Witnesses in Madagascar, somebody dressed like a native would announce the report; the same for Bolivia or Eskimo land. We had some demos with lights out and everything played out in florescent-painted hands, feet and faces. They got to be so sensational that word must have reached headquarters. "That's California for you" got to be a saying from Brooklyn Heights to the Gulf of Mexico. Probably the limit was reached when some of the Service Meetings were conducted entirely by the young ones, including opening and concluding prayer. These were years of growth of our families in the spiritual realm. It remains a period that still affords pleasant, though sometimes laughable memories. It also reminds me of a state of affairs mentioned more that once in the book of Judges: "As for everybody, what was right in his own eyes he was accustomed to do." Our congregation of course was not the only one trying to out rival Hollywood. Word eventually came out in our *Kingdom Service* monthly informant that the intent of our programs was education more than entertainment and so do not overplay the parts.

Still a lot of creative activity was going on, generating excitement. At assemblies Volunteer Service afforded outlets for just about anything you could do ---21 departments I think it was--- from First Aid to Trucking, Live Orchestra, News Service. At outside sports stadiums there were erected colossal tents to shelter the Kitchen and Dining areas. Full course meals were served from scratch and people were fed on assembly lines, 20,000 an hour or more. The Military and mass control agencies came to study how Jehovah's Witnesses managed it. We attended the last big International Convention in New York that attracted a quarter million people from 53 countries. It spilled over both Yankee Stadium and the Polo Grounds. Eight days it lasted, with sessions running from nine to nine, twelve hours a day.

The Rooming department had canvassed a hundred miles square searching for rooms in private homes. We drove from California in the station wagon, sleeping in it along the way. When we got to the City in the middle of the night and managed to find our way around Gotham, our hotel room by that time had been given to someone else. One more night in the station wagon. I'd hate to sleep in New York nowadays in a station wagon.

Anyway, Jehovah's Witnesses have expanded earth wide by so many millions it is unthinkable to hold a world convention anywhere on the planet.

OUR firstborn, John, cut his teeth on aviation. As soon as he could toddle he went to the airport with me where I was instructing. He waddled about, many times with wet diapers dragging while I finished a student lesson. He himself flew when he was ten, and soloed at 16, became a commercial licensed pilot and flight instructor at 18. Most of the time for his commercial license he got with me as copilot while on a charter to Las Vegas. It was what we called the Drunk Run. We would take some high timers there in the middle of the night from bars in Ontario and wait in Las Vegas outside the casinos for them to lose their money and bring them back. Many times when they were past sobering up, we would return without them.

Our second son Sam (his real name is Neil Steven) followed a similar course. He was almost born on a plane. He flew with me and the family through Mexico and elsewhere while still an infant.

John Leslie, three years older, was always a leader in his attempts. He had a sharp intellect, which I lay small claim to bequeathing. He adapted readily both to flying and the ground book work. Usually a person adapts either to the flying as a natural and avoids the books, or vice versa. But he took readily to both. At 17, now possessing his private pilot's license , he started taking his girlfriend for a ride and treating her to the stalls and other antics that bring forth more screams than a roller coaster. I thought so many, many times, Lord, if I was a mother of one of these girls, I'd forbid from now till doomsday to let her fly with a green kid of a pilot. But then I'd reflect back on my own escapade with Smiling Joe.

While John advanced with his commercial time building, Sam began logging his own pre-solo time. As I mentioned, John got most of his basic instruction during the Drunk Runs to Las Vegas. At l0,000 feet altitude inebriated passengers would fall asleep and I was free to instruct John in all the details. One night we got a wide awake drunk who'd had a lot of coffee and he leaned on the back of John's seat all the way, saying to me, "Now I don't want you to let this kid fly, see?" John didn't like it. To benefit from these midnight lessons he'd have to sacrifice sleeping time and next day at school he'd have to fight to stay awake. Most of the time, going and coming, John would do most of the flying, and sometimes I would join the snoozers and leave it to him.

Ontario was an alternate for LAX (Los Angeles International) in those days. When fog hit the coast, airliners packed Ontario like cars in a baseball stadium parking area. People milled around, frustrated, trying to find a cup of coffee. We put up signs all over the premises. "Flight to Burbank $l00." "To Palm Springs." " Vegas" Wherever. It was during these unscheduled flights that John got most of his hours logged for his commercial ticket. We scurried from trip to trip, helping folks make their destinations . Even so, sometimes we had balkers. They'd look at the little Cherokee, after stepping off a 707 and say, "Oh no, that's too little."

Meanwhile Sam and his buddies would round up sandwiches and coffee and make a killing selling at inflated prices to a captive market. After some days, of course the fog would lift and off the liners would go, so we had to do our thing the first few days.

Sam followed in John's footsteps and soloed various planes at 16 when he got his driver's license. The newspapers had a new story now, since Sam was taught by his brother instead of by his

Mom. By now I had my flying service at Chino Airport, so the boys got in some PR for Nickie's Flying School.

RUTH JOHNSON FLYING SERVICE was started at Chino after I was fired from Holiday Flying. My boss at Holiday and I had clashing ideas on treatment of students. So I simply took "my" students and rented a small room for $50 a month on the other end of the airport. My only plan at that time was to finish the course of the students who chose to stay with me. After that I could go on to find another job as chief pilot. However things did not work out that way. The owner of Holiday in my opinion was slightly bent out of shape. He had just built a half-million dollar operation, complete with buildings, offices, hangars and fuel facilities. Undertakings like that light up the dollar marks in the entrepreneur's eyes. And with ambition comes pride and arrogance. When Holiday announced our demise, prematurely, that was too much. Our stubborn streak showed through. A battle was joined. We stuck to our $50 hole in the wall. Two students, Walter Moreman and Ola Groover, had planes they were willing to lease to us. We started a fun flight operation. With my two sons I took on Holiday.

Swede, it so happened, still worked in maintenance for Holiday. When he would stop by to see his family we would suddenly hush and say "Shhhh,-- enemy ears" in exaggerated tones. That got the best of Swede. Despite lush offers to stay on as maintenance chief, he left Holiday and joined us at the West End. As for Holiday, they had lost not only their flight department but their maintenance management. We had the customers and the aircraft maintenance.

It was only surface triumph. It was the beginning of an undermining process that, once started, would prove to be eventual ruination for me.

For a time we became one of the most well known and best liked schools in the Valley. People came from miles around to fly from our school. We became state approved, FAA approved and VA (Veterans Administration) approved. We remained tops in popularity and prosperity until the "domino"* intervention in 1975.*(A GOVERMENT AGENT ON A CASE FOLLOWING A

PROCEDURE RATHER THAN THOUGHT)
From the start we were under fire from the competition.
Their complaints to the FAA, to the state school board and to
anyone else who might damage us, were nonstop and unrelenting.
We had to get all our credentials in order in record time, and never
relax our vigilance.

We would not have survived the early beginnings had it not
been for an attorney, Mr. Tobin. I had met him while at Ontario.
Attorney Tobin chose to resume his flight training with us at
Chino. He saw the pressures being engineered by Holiday. For
instance, the County of San Bernadino, which leased to Holiday,
was defending their potentially profitable lease-holder against
little me. Mr. Tobin was somewhat a maverick attorney who
relished fighting for rights. He had money and a right motive. He
fought the cause for me. I could trade him flying time and trips
against his fees. I will always be indebted to him. It was plain to
see that from the time my operation started in 1968 until it ended in
a shambles ten years later, I should have had a lawyer for a
partner.

Chapter 14

A TASTE OF NEW WORLD JOYS

DURING the 1960's we had the adventure of attending the European conventions. Times were hard at that point, as Swede had lost his job. But when the day came we packed the old stationwagon and left for Ohio. There we dropped off the kids with grandparents. Swede's relatives were impressed that he was able to make a trip to Europe, thinking he must be high in some company. At Philadelphia we met our charter flight, an Imperial Airlines plane. This was a Constellation, definitely not a modern jet. We were taken the northern route to Europe, because of the needed gas stops at Newfoundland, Greenland and then Ireland . It was a long, uneventful trip, with not much sleep in the rough air of the North Atlantic. We landed in beautiful green Ireland. My Mom would be elated that one Irish member of our family made the trek.

In London we took a cab and shuddered in the back seat as the driver, sitting on the right side, wound in and out of traffic. We arrived at the home where we were to stay and were greeted by a middle-age English couple who seemed surprised to see us. We learned later that they had placed bets on our age and both lost, as they were counting on an older retired couple.

They immediately wanted to know what kind of work Swede did, assuming of course that I was a housewife and nothing more. When Swede told them he was in the aircraft industry they thought we were rich. They thought all Americans were rich, Swede said, and nuts too.

London was different for Swede from his days in the Fourth Fighter Group. He'd look around and shake his head. "It's hard to believe Hitler was trying to bomb London off the map. The nights were blackouts. The only lights you saw were bombs exploding all over town."

Outside of a few routine tourist sights, our time was spent at the Convention sessions. We were glad every time they had an

American speaker, as we had a lot of problems with the "English" English. American English is a language on its own. When Marley Cole's book, *JEHOVAH'S WITNESSES The New World Society,* came out in the English version he was amazed. "I thought I was writing somewhat standard English," he said, "even though bits of Tennessee vernacular crept in unawares. But when I saw how the British publishers rewrote the text I wondered who wrote the original."

As we were crossing the English Channel Swede recalled that when he was flying to Germany many who had been shot up did not make it back, but went into the Channel, and had five minutes to be rescued before they would freeze in the icy waters. He barely made it once, to land with Djligooblie's tail shot up.

The Netherlands was all aflower and the canals were fascinating, and my introduction to flea markets was in Holland.

Because the conventions were in multiple languages you could sit in the one that used your language.

From there we went to Hamburg, Germany, by train. This convention was huge, the kind of sight that if Hitler could have seen it he would have died on the spot. We stayed with a young German couple who ran a movie theater. They had a car, which they said was their choice over having a child. They could afford only one or the other. They could not speak English. We could not speak German. Conversation was hard to come by.

People came from all over Europe and many parts of the world. Some older ladies pedaled bicycles hundreds of miles. There were brothers and sisters there who had escaped out of Communist East Germany at the risk of their lives, just to attend the convention. They had not seen so much as a song book. It stirred pangs in your heart to realize how much we in a country like the US. took for granted.

How those people ate at the cafeteria! Swede and I could not begin to eat all they served.

We walked through portions of the city that had been bombed by the B-17's that Swede had escorted in his P51. Much had never been rebuilt. It seemed to have a profound effect on Swede and me too. "I actually had a hand in this carnage, in ruining this city and killing these people. It happened right here in our generation. We are in a country where there were forced-labor camps and concentration camps and extermination camps. Millions of Jews and Poles and Slavs and Gypsies and Jehovah's Witnesses were destroyed in Hitler's Holocaust. Who wants more proof that Satan the Devil is the God of this world?"

It made Swede sick, a sickness I shared. "Here we were, maybe twenty thousand Witnesses who refused to fight for Hitler. And what did 40 million Lutherans and 20 million Catholics do? Would Hitler have had an army without them?" He gagged. "To think that before I learned the truth, I thought it was grand and glorious to do the same thing! How each side in any and every war justifies itself. *Justifies itself!* "

It made you a little nervous just to walk down the street toward the convention grounds, as if the very earth under your feet was sick too. In some way never so real before, you realized the Creator and Owner of this earth is looking down, poised in this generation to bring to ruin those ruining his planet, and you are thankful in your heart that you were joining company with the one society of people out of all nations who have beaten their swords into plowshares.

In the vast stadium with tens of thousands of your brothers and sisters gathered round you, all sharing in the wonderful news that at last it is time for God's Kingdom to begin operating in the midst of its enemies, to bring real peace and unity across all racial and national and religious barriers, where everyone knows what it means to beat swords into plowshares---In this gathering there were veterans of all the wars of Christendom and pagandom who would never again point a gun at each other. If tens of thousands can find this peace, why can't tens of millions? If millions can find it, why can't billions? We were demonstrating it for all the world to see.

After we landed back in Philadelphia, I took a picture of our plane, the old Constellation. Before I got my roll of film developed I would see another picture of this plane---at its crash site in Tennessee. It went down with a load of football players.

Chapter 15

DISFELLOWSHIPPED

THE spiritual euphoria of those wonderful conventions in Europe soon turned bittersweet in my heart. Just when we as a family seemed to be broadening our horizon, things took a turn. A turn for the worse for me.

I had started my own business all over again. Between my love of flying and the exertion demanded for running a flight operation, my energies were expended. It was the old battle of trying to serve two masters and losing out to the wrong one. My master became flight operations, complex operations involving a designated flight examiner of the FAA, which I was now, besides holding a government charter and FAA to operate an airline to Baja, and managing a Veteran Flight School.

Swede meantime showed more growth in Godly love, wisdom, justice and power. He kept his balance. He put in minimum hours in our maintenance operation, then off he went to his theocratic duties. His shepherding efforts toward me were thwarted by my resistant course of involvement with managers and employees. You tell yourself your involvement is only temporary, and we need money so bad, and soon we'll have things under control and our money problems will be over---after all, the Bible says "money is for a protection". The process of slipping away can be subtle. You tell yourself it's only a hump ahead. But the hump grows into a hill and the hill into a mountain.

Your senses become dulled to the fact that Bible truths pull you toward a new life, a life apart from this system of things absorbed in everyday anxieties. Bible truths draw you into a new association with like-minded persons, persons apart, responding to new principles, new guidelines, new works, new aspirations, a new destiny---a society of people actually expecting to survive this world's end into an earthly Paradise.

This new mode of life, unprecedented since Noah and his family survived a world's end, takes dedication and devotion to associating with fellow believers in prayer and study and meetings and in the public service of teaching publicly and from house to house like the first-century Christians did. Oh I knew all that, yes in the example of my own household, my husband, and even my two young sons.

It reminded me of the circumstances some of my old gambling charter customers got themselves into; they got all their chips out on the table, and they had to keep backing them up, down to the last chip, and then the oblivion of drink. My meeting attendance became "When I can make it." My ministry became token service, two or three hours a month, out of compulsion, not out of appreciation for having the hope of life. My spirituality dwindled as my associations with this worldly employee group increased.

We would gather in the evenings after work, in the Orange Room, and round- table our problems of the day, and flush them out, for the moment, with bourbon and soda. Or else we would all go over to a local restaurant.

What complicated matters all the more was Ray. Ray was a Witness, or had been. But Ray lacked the spiritual strength to resist worldly influence. He was my school manager. Under this constant exposure to the smoke filled room, Ray fell back to smoking.

"Why make a big deal out of smoking?" Ray would say to the elders.

They would have him read 2 Corinthians 7:l: "Since we have these promises, beloved ones, let us cleanse ourselves of every defilement of flesh and spirit."

Ray would dispute that tobacco defiles the flesh. His defense was, like an alcoholic, "I can quit any time I want to."

He never wanted to. They'd have him read the "greatest" command: "You must love Jehovah with your whole heart and with your whole soul and your whole mind."

"I do that," he declared.

"You have no mental reservations about the truth?"

"No."

"Or emotional reservations?"

"No,"

"With your heart and mind you love Jehovah unreservedly?"

"Sure."

"But what about your soul, your whole breathing living being, your flesh?"

His "soul" was enslaved to tobacco. The flesh , if enslaved to anything, defiles the heart and mind. Maybe Ray couldn't see that, or didn't want to see it. Eventually he was disfellowshipped.

That imperiled me, too. Now I had a disfellowshipped member in my management group.

Swede, a responsible overseer in the congregation, tried heart and soul to dissuade me from the course down which I was headed.

"Stop nagging me!" I fired back. "If you want to help, get in here and relieve the work load."

"You know what I'm talking about, Nickie. The apostle Paul warns us to quit mixing in company with anyone called a brother that is not a brother, not even eating with such a man."

"I'm not eating with Ray. I'm only having a drink."

"You mean Ray's not there when the whole bunch goes to eat?"

I didn't answer. Of course Ray was there.

"You're not helping Ray," Swede pointed out. "You're making him feel it doesn't matter to be disfellowshipped. How is he ever going to see the need to stop befouling the life God gave him?"

I had reviewed Ray's record before hiring him. He was an ex-con who'd been sentenced to Chino men's' prison for writing bad checks. Murderers there were getting out in seven years and bank robbers at much less. Ray's record indicated that he was a promoter who sometimes over-promoted. I felt he'd been handed a raw deal. I gave him a job.

Ray's assignment, besides being school manager, was to take care of the dogs and the yard, including a trailer I had rented at the airport.   Not the least of his duties was to beat off inspectors. He was perfect for the job. He had a glib tongue and a rough mouth, and was totally unimpressed by a badge. One run-in I wished he had not had, was with " Sweet Lue", as I called her out of malice. Lue was the bookkeeper and after I fired her, due to her resentment of both Ray and me, she spilled all kinds of dirt to the FBI and that brought Monda down on me.

But before all that, there were some heady times, thanks in large part to Ray. It was obvious that his intellect soared above average. He had definite aptitudes in planning. I appointed him dispatcher in the flight office. Immediately he promoted and increased the flight school. He planned fly-ins and barbecues. Our school became the most popular of many airports and the students flocked in. We had promotion parties, commercial hangar weekend conventions at Chino Airport, where flying products and accessories in the Valley were on exhibition. All these promotions were by Ray, and I was enthused. Here was a man with foresight in aviation marketing.

We even organized an airport Association with other fixed base operators, and had an air show, which is to this day copied by other organizations on the airports. At times we rented planes from neighboring airports. Other operators tried to copy our ideas and style, but they didn't seem to meet with our success. We had the telling combination. We became known in all the Southern California area as the friendly school. Our instructors were all natural pilots, with a deep interest in their students. And students stood in line and vied to get on the schedule.

This type of success is the kind you lose yourself in, heart, mind and soul. And it is also a target for the competition, for the envious, the jealous, and the ones with an ax to grind. We never knew who the real enemy was who started the false reports. But inspections and investigations multiplied. From then on it was an endless and uphill battle. The tide changed with waves of oncoming dominos from local, state and Federal authorities.

Swede kept distancing himself farther and farther from the business. I, instead of walking away from a losing tide, stubbornly fought on. I could not believe it would go on forever, this mean-natured opposition. How simple it would have been to sell my interests, fold my tent and be on my way like a discreet person. No, I had to fight. I saw my troubles as nothing else but the Devil tormenting me.

What *was* real was that I was seen having meals in a downtown restaurant with a disfellowshipped person. With Ray of course. Swede conveniently planned a trip to the Ozarks, to "look around". That left me without a maintenance supervisor. All this happened in conjunction with my being called in by the elders.

I could have been tactful and explained my position, altered my course, anything but what I did. I was mad at the world, at my husband, feeling persecuted and misjudged, strained by pressures from all sides. I went down to the Orange Room, fortified myself with a couple of quick courage belts of bourbon, and went to my meeting with the elders.

These brothers were kind. They had known me for years. They loved our family and held my husband in deep respect. They pleaded with me to change my attitude. In their view they were being more than understanding and merciful.

To me they were asking too much. I politely told them to stay out my business and let me alone.

"Are you leaving us no recourse?"

"Do what you have to do," I retorted, and walked out.

The only recourse I left them was to disfellowship.

Chapter 16

ALONE

IN l970 John met and fell in love with Joy Lynn Hill. Her folks, shortly after that, moved back to their home place in Cassville MO, in the Ozarks. How does the Song of Songs express it?-- "Many waters are not able to extinguish love." John arranged a flight with a customer east to that area, and then fell in love with a second beauty, life in the Ozarks. If rivers themselves cannot wash it away, neither could I. I lost my chief flight instructor. The wedding, which I insisted upon, had to take place in California, in our hangar. Over 500 guests regaled themselves with champagne and congratulations to the bride and groom who were to fly off that night on their honeymoon.

John was replaced by my number two son, Sam, who was number two in age only. Sam endeared himself to his students. Sam endeared himself to everyone, and that was the problem. He chose his vacation time in the winter, mainly because a Californian has limited experience with a winter wonderland. Sam went to the Ozarks Mountains to see the snow. And to visit his brother.

The real attraction, I was confounded to learn, was a little dark-haired beauty named Julie. Julie was a sister to John's wife, Joy Lynn. This made her Sam's sister-in-law. Sam's intent was to change the relationship. When he married Julie that made his brother his brother-in-law. Julie's sister became her sister-in-law. It sounded like some version of a patriarchal family. One time I asked John how it felt to be the leader of this pack of brothers and sisters and husbands and wives. He said it felt something like a two-way marriage. In time the addition of little Brandi and Lacey to John's household, and Sally and Joel to Sam's, turned brothers into uncles and sisters into aunts to each other's clans, and mothers and fathers were treated alike by the young ones who were more like brothers and sisters than cousins.

John and Sam never left the Ozarks. Neither did Swede. I was the only holdout.

I drugged myself on work to block out the thoughts of being alone.

The boys tried for awhile to pursue a life of aviation there in southern Missouri. I gave them an airplane to use, a Cessna l50. In that area there were not enough aviation aspirants. They had to turn to a more lucrative livelihood and became stone masons. With this they met success. Flying with them is now only a pastime.

Swede knew loneliness, but not the loneliness I knew. He, after all, was with our family. Both our fleshly family and our spiritual family. I was with no one. Except Ray. I was never sure if Ray truly sensed the deeper estrangement, the loss of our relationship with our spiritual family and our "Father of lights", Jehovah. I don't think Ray ever comprehended mentally what it meant to be spiritually dedicated. I know that was a question that plagued me. It was hard to take personally the Scripture that says "It would have been better for them not have known the path of righteousness than after knowing it accurately to turn away from the holy commandment delivered to them." How accurately did I know the path of righteousness? It was somehow inconceivable to think the rest of that Scripture applied to me: "The saying of the true proverb has happened to them: 'The dog has returned to its own vomit, and the sow that was bathed to rolling in the mire'."

What pierces like daggers is that your knowledge of the truth, your understanding of the words of life, stays with you. Knowledge is one thing. Wisdom is another. Wisdom is the use of knowledge. You can forsake wisdom. Knowledge is still with you. If you have a conscience still, knowledge is there to torment it.

You find yourself seeking outlets, quirky thrills and excitement, anything to blot out your thoughts. You seek ways to die. In my album of pilots that I treasure, there was this special friend, Larry Hill. He flew the B17 bomber out of Chino that dropped borate on the fires that sometimes ate up the California hills. I managed after some persuasion for Larry to let me stow away in the glass nose of his plane and watch the fires boil up from below. It was a kind of cloak-and-dagger stunt in the first place to sneak on the plane at the end of the runway at Chino, away from the eyes of the Forestry Department officials. But once Larry

73

got underway it was a death-defying adventure to shrivel up there in mortal terror in the glass nose while Larry swooped down on the flames. It required the utmost respect and admiration for the pilot as he vaulted in and out of box canyons with his load and make drops in the smoke and flame. It would not have been more than expected had he crashed nose- first into one of those infernos, and I never really asked myself if I would have cared.

It may strike you as preposterous that a religious society in which the concern for one another is founded on 'no greater love than this, that one lay down his life for a friend'----it may seem out of kilter that such a society will as readily banish one for smoking along with one who fraternizes with the smoker. Jehovah's Witnesses have been dealt with harshly over such issues. I feel I am somewhat qualified to respond. Never did I in the darkest hour feel unjustly judged. The committee of elders who dealt with my situation applied no personal rules. Neither did the Watchtower Society which sponsors and oversees the congregations. The Society, which claims no inspiration nor infallibility, points out what they understand to be the Bible principle to the elders and the elders point out the principle to the one involved. it was up to me how I accepted it, whether as a narrow minded religious judgment , or "not as the word of men, but just as it truthfully is, as the word of God". If Jehovah is to have a clean people, he has to l) provide them clean guidelines, and 2) they must respect the guidelines. If any feel the principles are too restrictive, well, we can declare our rights. I had done that. Rights might be fine if we didn't need protection from them. Rights pretty much boil down to freedom to reap what we sow. I can site you two well learned Scriptures on that: Galatians 6:5 and Deuteronomy 30:l9.

**B17 BOMBER
DROPPING BORATES ON
FIRE IN THE
CALIFORNIA HILLS**

Chapter 17

MR. MONDA

THE end is seldom foreseen from the beginning. The beginning may be too subtle for foresight. But from hindsight it appears that the unraveling might have started with trying to do a favor for the Baldy View ROP---Regional Occupational Program. ROP had to do with training high school students in practical skills, including aviation. This favor involved a flight exhibition at Montclair Plaza. They wanted to know if I would consider landing my Piper Club there for a display. I said I would survey the situation.

We got permission from the local sheriff's department and the manager of the Plaza to overfly the Plaza early in the morning to see if there would be sufficient area to land and take off. I left it with the ROP to get the permits. Now notice I said *"I left it with the ROP to get the permits"*. That shortcoming of mine, leaving details up to others because details suffocate me, that shortcoming of mine would be noted as my undoing years later in a report when my very life hung in the balance. Well, the ROP got the permits all right, except they overlooked the one that counted most, the one from the mighty FAA. So I plodded out of bed inspite of a bad cold, got into the breezy cab, and proceeded to the Plaza, where I surveyed the situation from about 500 feet, or as close as you could estimate from the insensitive altimeter of a 1946 aircraft.

Of course there would be some sharp-eyed custodian of law who spotted the yellow Cub hovering over the Plaza and who forthrightly alerted the FAA.

There was a hearing, naturally. The FAA's witnesses were deputy sheriffs who didn't know their department had approved the flight and whose knowledge of aviation was watching airliners land and depart from some airport. We lost the case and all the subsequent appeals.

While under suspension Ray remodeled the county hangars and made them look respectable. We took on dealerships and won prizes in selling aircraft. Then he promoted an airline to Baja. It was at a time when people were afraid to venture south of the border because of the change of presidents in Mexico. There was some uprising between the peasants and the have-it-alls, and this gained great publicity.

Ray said the time was ripe to establish an airline to Baja. He outlined just how to go about it and I followed his formula to a T. It was Ray's great gift to lay out formulas. But somebody else always had to carry them out.

I got my favorite reporter from *The Los Angeles Times*, some fishermen, my Beechcraft, my captain's uniform, my co-pilot, and off we went to Loreto. The reporter came up with a feature and pictures on the whole expedition. When it came out in the VIEW section, about this gal who flies a party of sports into bandito country without incident, and they come up with a fabulous catch of tuna, well the passengers started to roll, and we put tourism back into Baja in the next several months. We established our line, paving the way for several US lines that are flying to Baja today.

The FAA's temporary suspension gave us the very thing we needed, a breathing spell during which to revitalize our operations. But in the midst of it all, Ray met with an accident in Mazatlan, Mexico. He fell off a touring bus and fractured his skull. It was while he was promoting a resort with a ranch owner, a resort for fiesta flights. We brought him back and he was put in intensive care where it was touch and go for awhile. But he even promoted himself past the Devil, as he put it, and finally came out of it. However the Mazatlan sidewalk had left its mark permanently; blackouts were frequent, and he was visibly suffering. He became gaunt, and he increased his drinking habits to offset the pain.

How wide and deep the chasm had breached between one Nickie Carter and a galaxy of bureaucracies became apparent the day Mr. Monda walked in. He was a chubby little man who reminded me of Winston Churchill. Only when he walked up close and fixed you with that grin, it was not cherubic. It was icy, like his slate-gray eyes. Another man accompanied him. I was to learn that Mr. Monda never ventured alone.

"Dale Monda with the FBI," he said cryptically, and flashed his badge. "Give me your school records. I have a subpoena."

My attorney friend, Art Black, was there. Art was a VA student. He immediately got to his feet in my defense. "We will give up no records," Art told him. "They remain at the school."

Mr. Monda never knew that Art Black was not my attorney. But Art handled things with full authority, even excusing me to go ahead with a scheduled flight exam.

THAT was the beginning of three years of surveillance by Mr. Monda. He interviewed all my students as to their courses and schedules. At first the students were indignant, for me and the school they really loved. They complained to the Veterans Administration and the VA, in collusion with the FHA, told them to enroll in another school. All the while Mr. Monda was working on them. The VA meanwhile cut off my school benefits, still owing me $26,000 in earned student fees. While Mr. Monda was wearing them down the VA assured them that when they enrolled in another school their benefits would start all over again. To escape the harassment the students did what they were told. They were not in this to champion me against Federal bureaucracies but to learn to fly and get their ratings.

I recovered for awhile by getting a Small Business Administration loan. With that money I bought a D18 Beechcraft. On the basis of that equipment I was able to win a Navy contract. The idea became a dream of vengeance within me to play one Federal system against another.

But what a comedown. For that first commercial flight I donned my captain's uniform and proudly boarded the plane to fly to Miramar Naval Base, the first sendoff on the contract. The naval crews were kind of thrilled to have a woman pilot. We had a gala sendoff. News media, cameras and the commanders greeting us on arrival.

My contract called for one cargo flight a day. One week later I was confronted by a schedule four times beyond what the bid covered. End of contract and beginning of payments on an SBA loan I couldn't meet.

Chino Airport is little if any different from other small airports. The pilots spend five hours on the ground for every one in the air. There's plenty of time for hangar gossip. I had grown so hypersensitive and combative I imaged there was only one subject of discussion and that was me and my shadows. I know for a fact that I was accused of everything from marijuana trips across the border, to hauling aliens, guns, tropical birds and on and on. I should have been a multi-millionairess trouncing around in my Lear jet, or a name lost in some prison in Southern California or northern Mexico.

Ray went to Mexico for about six months to try ranching. He purchased some land that was not owned by the seller (it was quite a pastime in Mexico). And of course the investment was lost.

He came back penniless. Within twelve hours Mr. Monda trounced him. He charged Ray with raising marijuana instead of lettuce. Mr. Monda left without a confession, but bruised and angered by the glib barbs he brought down on himself.

My chief ground school instructor, who always appointed himself my benefactor, after several sessions with Mr. Monda, came to me and proposed that I turn Ray in. If I would, the whole investigation the VA was pushing would be dropped. The dominos were getting nervous, in need of at least a fall guy.

But I had nothing to turn Ray in for. This time they were charging that Ray had kited the books. Ray had nothing to do with the books. "Sweet Lou" was the bookkeeper.

Meanwhile the airport manager, under prodding, tried every tactic imaginable to get me out of the airport. The outrage was suffocating. If somebody had come along with a Bible and cited something about leaving rage alone and stop showing yourself heated up, and if he had added to that the wrath of man (or woman) does not work out God's righteousness, I would have told him where to go and how high to jump. I couldn't see that the Devil had me where he wanted me, trying to battle him in my own strength.

RUTH JOHNSON FLYING SERVECE & PIPER COMANCHE

AIRLINE TO BAJA

I was at the airport seven days a week, scrounging to stay afloat. With limited students I no longer had a school. I had to abandon my Mexican flying of real estate investors which I had developed at Guaymas. The contract went to another airline.

The county had given Ray such a rough time because of Mr. Monda's investigation that he was unable to conduct any business. "As long as the county is doing the harassing, it might as well support the harassee," Ray decided. I drove him down to apply for welfare. He got food stamps. I applied too. I got fifty bucks a month for rent for the trailer which the inspectors seemed to occupy more than I did.

Chapter 18

DESOLATION

IT had been two years since I set foot in a Kingdom Hall. The isolation from my family, the loneliness, the despair from struggling with the business and trying to combat insuperable odds, and most of all that sense that you know God but are estranged from Him, no one knows how heavily it weighs on the heart until he suffers it. Banishment. I felt like Cain. Cain murdered his brother. For that crime God banished him. "My punishment for error is too great to carry," Cain said. I had not killed anyone but I had spurned spiritual authority. Banishment was getting too great a load to carry.

Finally I mustered the courage to go to a meeting. I would talk to the brothers and try to get information on how to handle a comeback if possible. At that time it did not seem too clear on how to go about it.

Afterward it was pointed out to me by an older and seasoned overseer that two mistakes were made to start with. First, a Kingdom Hall meeting with the congregation present is not the time or place for a discussion this private and serious. Second, whoever is approached should arrange a meeting when all involved can meet in private. Problems of life and death seriousness can hardly be resolved in a few minutes before or after a scheduled public meeting.

Unfortunately for me none of the brothers were there who knew me previously. The one I approached turned me over to a young, new elder.

While others were still in conversational groups throughout the Hall, he took me to a front row seat. I felt on-stage. The young elder in an abrupt manner began a thrust of questions. What about my associates? How long since my husband left me? Why were we separated? It was, to me, cold, no empathy, no commendation for making an attempt to come back, but more like putting up the unwelcome sign. I left, vowing never to come back. I never did.

It was the kind of experience that disposes a person of my temperament, as it prevailed at that time, to start elder bashing. The modern elder arrangement was instituted during the early '70's. "The apostle Paul says elders are appointed by holy spirit," an old overseer told me. "Some of us felt the appointment was like getting a shot of holy spirit from some kind of spiritual syringe. If we were full of holy spirit how could we be wrong about anything?" Then he added: "In reality the appointment comes about by a man's spiritual maturity being recognized beforehand. His appointment is a confirmation of what is already observed by all, and now he is responsible for exercising his advancement in behalf of the congregation." One more thing he added: "He does not become inspired or infallible. Jehovah's Witnesses from the Governing Body on down are not infallible. We're Bible students."

I said, "Elders like to remind us that Isaiah 32:2 applies to them, that they are a shelter from the storm."

"But read the first six words of that verse. I read: *"And each must prove to be."*

Chapter 19

ARREST

AS soon as my employees got wind of the bankruptcy proceedings, it was like some one hollering "raid" in a house of ill repute. Things disappeared like magic. You'd look for a tool and it wasn't there. A radio, where was it? The calculator? At night, I was told, they would back up their trucks and load up. By the time the papers were filled out and filed and accepted, the inventory and equipment were reduced 75 percent. The SBA was furious at the inventory count. The bank that made the loan was screaming rape. Poor Stan, the loan officer, that was his first loan. And he was pushing for bank manager.

I lost my airline to Baja, not to mention my reputation. It seemed that Friend Monda visited every airport in the Valley or wherever we landed, to inquire had they seen Nickie's airplanes? Was there any sign of marijuana? Aliens? Guns? Illegal cargo? Those who knew me well would ask what in the world was I up to? Those who didn't know me wondered how one person had the guts to do all those things. Stories spread. The National Racing Champion was outdoing the banditos in Baja.

With the bankruptcy went my FAA examiner rating, my flight school, my would-be friends, my students, my livelihood. I barely hung on to my pilot's license to scrape by.

I HAD just returned from a delightful convention of the *WASP* "Order of Fifinella" at Colorado Springs. These were held every two years. But I had not been to the last two. Hoping to get away for at least a gasp of fresh air, I had made up my mind to go to this one. The therapy worked. I was feeling like old times, memories reawakened by the reunion.

This morning I was enjoying a sleep-in at my apartment at Chino Airport. I had put up a security fence and locked gate around my little building.

What woke me was the sound of my name being paged outside the gate. The voice was unmistakable. Short, staccato, running the words together: "Mrs. --Johnson?" Gone pleasant memories in less than a heartbeat. Through a peephole I saw Mr. Monda trailed by a man and a woman.

Maybe he was coming to talk about the letter I had written to his boss, Mr. Burton. Now that letter was the most ill-advised mistake I ever made. It had been proposed, with all the best intentions, by my old friend Bud Kagen. For three years Mr. Monda's inquisition had been going on. Bud suggested that I list all the details in a letter to Mr. Monda's superior.

What a fool. Do you expect a mother lion to turn on her cub?

Still wrapped in my robe I made an effort to be civil and invited them in. Mr. Monda's approach was to come directly at you, confrontation style. For the first time the grin was not icy. He was flushed triumphantly. "You said in your letter, Mrs. Johnson, that this investigation has gone on long enough. I agree. We are through with it. You are under arrest."

I went into shock. No matter how long you anticipate it, you really don't know how you'll react till it hits you. If Ray had not happened to drive up at that moment, no one might have known what happened to me.

Mr. Monda had planned the arraignment to take place in Orange County. This was not the county where I conducted business. It made things all the more complicated for me. Mr. Monda's male cohort gave Ray the address in Orange and I was able to give him my checkbook to arrange bail. I also called my attorney.

Mr. Sackey, my attorney, was in Los Angeles on a deposition at the time. "Why that double-crosser," he swore under his breath. "Monda had assured me that if it ever came to this, I would be notified ahead and we would talk to the authorities together."

Mr. Sackey beat us to the Orange County Federal Building and got to the magistrate first. He had convinced the magistrate, due to my having been in the community 25 years, to release me on my own recognizance. Then, before I was brought in, Mr. Monda got to the magistrate . He was pulling for $15,000 bail. The willywashy magistrate, between his commitment to Mr. Sackey and his awe of Mr. Monda, compromised at $10,000. Off to the pokey I went.

With my one phone call I informed Ray. It was one devilish chore for Ray. He finally managed with the efforts of a friend who had an in with the Teamster's Union.

Meanwhile I was getting acquainted with my cell-mates in the holding tank. There was a variety ranging from toughies to gals stoned on drugs. Some hookers had been pulled off the streets at the moment of transacting business. There were welfare cheats and there were some who had been there so many times it was to them like old home week. Most were having a nicotine fit, with cigarettes flashing like fireflies through blue smog.

The cold, that soul-chilling cold felt only in a prison, that along with the hours of waiting with no news, the coming out of the shock of arrest, of knowing at long last your time has come and everybody, maybe including Ray, has forsaken you, the intolerable anticipation of nothing but the worst-- I tried to tell myself there were worst fates. But I couldn't think of any.

I have faced impending death in an airplane. There was the time I was ferrying a T6 through the overcast in the Appalachians. The pilot tube froze and I lost my altimeter and airspeed. Only guesswork can control an airplane without these instruments. At any second you could bore into a mountain. Nothing like the panic then compared to this restriction behind gray iron bars. And that time before an operation when the doctor said, "Without blood more than likely you will die." I said, "So be it," and felt nothing like this cold insensitive loss of my very being.

The thought of a husband and family flitted through my mind, but they belonged to a life I had forfeited. I closed the door harshly on the thought. It was more bearable to think about why a confinement cell so terrorized me. It must be the mental horror of restriction, of having the wings clipped right off your free spirit. I watched the movements of the creatures in the holding tank, and then the activities of the workers outside the bars, working for the institution. On ene side there were humans have dominion, life and dèath control. On the other side, living things in human form creatures under dominion. No feeling in between. It is the horrible realization that once inside, you lose your identity, you no longer count as a human. No sense of mercy, no heart, no recognition as a fellow human being. The system is soul-shattering. I tried to pray but felt condemned. A verse from Isaiah kept damning me: "When you spread out your palms, I hide my eyes from you."

Eons replaced hours before my bail bondsman appeared with the magic document which I signed. As I was leaving the girls begged me to make phone calls, leave money for cigarettes, or whatever. At the checkout window I tried to leave what money I had. Momentarily I had forgotten; the system has no heart, no room for compassion. The effort was refused.

As I walked out with my liberators into the fresh air I breathed long and deep. Ray and the lawyer stood there, looking at me.

"Air and freedom," I said. "Never again will I take them for granted."

On October 10 I was to appear for the indictment. "A simple matter-of-fact procedure," Mr. Sackey assured. "You'll get a trial date and be assigned a judge."

An assigned judge and a trial date are anything but simple. On October 10 I would learn why. After receiving the indictment and my attorney was reading it, I was whisked into the holding area for more fingerprints and pictures. While they were trying to get the fingerprint machine to work and looking for a new bulb for the camera, someone came yelling for "Johnson!" (my married name) and waving papers .

"You're under arrest," he said. I went into post arrest shock.

"But I've not been indicted yet--"

"This charge's got nothing to do with that."

That's all he told me. My head was spinning in delirium. Back to the slammer. Would it mean another bail bond? If so, poor Ray would not be able to come through this time. I would be in jail God only knew how long.

I was meeting new cell mates. "Weren't you here last year?" one girl said.

This might have been the first time in my life when I was not able to utter a word. I stared blankly through the bars at the domino aids passing bologna sandwiches to everybody in the holding tank. From the brassy chatter going on around me it appeared there was a difference out there. They had arrested some guy who had money and influence. They tried the owner-slave treatment on him. When he got out he filed a class action suit against the city and won. After that inmates were getting regular meals and bologna sandwich breaks in between.

Not that I had a stomach for bologna sandwiches. Evelyn my secretary and Mr. Sackey and Ray and I had planned lunch in Chinatown after my so-called quickie indictment procedure was supposed to be over.

Why was I re-arrested? Mr.Monda had gotten my bail raised from $10,000 back to $15,000.

The arresting officer told me that it worked to my benefit that the fingerprint machine broke down and the camera wouldn't work. Because of this delay I had not appeared before my assigned judge for a trial date. He, the officer, was supposed to arrest me as I would have left the courtroom. That way the judge would already have been finished with me and gone. I would have had to sit in jail awaiting a new appearance. That could have taken the good Lord only knows how many days or weeks or...

After hours I was brought out to appear for a trial date. My attorney asked for a reduction of bail back to $10,000. The judge granted this as the plaintiff did not object and Mr. Monda was not present.

But in the process of being released I had to be returned to the holding tank. This process can drain your liver dry. With nothing better to do the dominos seem to sit and figure how to prolong things. At last a domino jangled his keys. All the girls fell silent. He opened the door and beckoned. It was for me.

As I walked out he said, "This is not your day, Johnson."

"Are you telling me!" But I didn't get his meaning.

"You have a ticket on the computer and we have to send you over to county jail for booking."

All hullabaloo broke out from the holding tank.

"A ticket?---I never got one in Los Angeles--I never go there!"

"Sorry. We have to send for the police. They will come over and you can find out what it's all about." We were nearly back to the checkout window. "It is late, though, almost 4:30," he added. "They'll probably just book you tonight and wait for tomorrow."

It struck then, like a thunderbolt. I *could* imagine a fate worse than the Orange County holding tank. That was the horror of the Los Angeles County jail.

Even Mr. Sackey was in shock. They were saying I would probably go to Sybil Brand for the night. The tales I had heard about that jail joint would shake this page.

It turned out that one domino had a shred of humanity. "Just sit quiet," he said. "If the police don't get here in fifteen minutes I'll release you to your attorney and he can take you over to pay your bail." He allowed Evelyn to slip me a check to write the $53.40 to cover the bail.

Twelve...thirteen...fourteen minutes crawled into eternity. He walked in then, a young fresh faced rookie, still partially unscathed by the system. On the drive over, you know what? We chatted about flying. He was a bigger enthusiast than Senor Portillo whom I hadn't come to know just yet. At the police station we chatted in the lobby. He did not even take me into the booking area. Dear Mr. Sackey arrived with the $53.40 cash. Again I was outside, tasting air. I did not even mind the smog. To this day I never found out what the charge was about. Who can blame me if I would have sworn with my hand on the Bible that it was one of Mr. Monda's dirtier tricks

Chapter 20

CONDEMNED

I WAS hoping it would be hush-hush about my arrest. But friends started sending in articles from newspapers in Ontario, Pomona, Orange County and Riverside. It practically destroyed my flying career. But not my fury. I stayed at the airport to face it.

My attorney was studying how to make the best defense. The plaintiff was bombarding him with plea bargaining proposals. A plea bargain, I came to learn, is generally when the defendant, that's me, offers to plead guilty to a lesser charge in exchange for the prosecution's dropping other charges. But in this case it appeared to be the other way around. The District Attorney was doing the pleading. "He knows he has a shaky case," Mr. Sackey said. "He wants somehow to guarantee a conviction."

That was the carrot he was holding out to me the donkey. But the stick he was holding over me was a full-size fence rail. The charges brought against me involved five aircraft I had sold. One was a Piper Cub which belonged to my husband Swede and son John. The other four were Piper aircraft. I was a Piper dealer and my arrangement was to maintain a rolling stock of four planes. As soon as one was sold Piper would replace it with another. I did not own the planes. I simply sold them as Piper's agent. But the way the charges were rigged, the SBA was supposed to hold a lien on the four craft I had sold.

The financing arrangements covering the sale of these four craft were not made with the SBA but with local banks. Only after consorting with the FBI were Federal liens filed. How this was manipulated don't ask me. I only know I was overshadowed with black clouds of threat hanging over me. The least count involved the Piper Cub I sold for my family for a measly $2,000, but was good for a $5,000 fine and five years you know where.

Now this plea bargaining arrangement was supposed to put an end to all threats hereafter. You sign a paper in which the plaintiff says so at the time---no more threats, no more hounding in court, no more charges, no more arrests involving this case---and that's the end. If you don't sign the paper, then you can't plea bargain later on. You face all five charges from now on, one after another. Arrests. Jails. Attorney fees. Trials. Prison terms. From here to Mr. Monda's grandchildren.

The catch is, to plea bargain means you admit to being guilty on at least this one charge. Mr. Sackey felt we could win on the one count as charged. But what about the forthcoming four? If I don't sign the paper and if I were super rich we could fight every one of them no matter how long it took, and demolish every trumped up charge they could come up with. So Mr. Sackey said. But he knew I didn't have the money.

"What is the one charge they want to bargain with?"

"That you sold one of those Piper airplanes for two thousand dollars."

"Well of course I sold that plane!" It made me furious. "Write out the paper. I'll sign it."

He wrote up the plea. "The charges against you are so flimsy, chances are ninety-eight percent that you'll get off scott-free or with probation, no jail. But just to make sure, I'm putting a lid of four months on jail time in case the dominos fall the very worst way."

Somehow when Mr. Sackey made me feel the worst was when he tried to sound the most optimistic. The judge assigned to my case, he said, was nicknamed Old Iron Horse, meaning he was fair (as a domino could be) but he was a "temperamental old cuss who sometimes comes off the wall with an oddball decision. So we need protection," as Mr. Sackey put it.

"You're writing it up so that even if Old Iron Horse has come off of some soured oats he can't send me up longer than four months?"

"That's right."

"But that was my family's plane!"

"They'll try to prove it was the SBA's"

AS we appeared in court on my trial date I felt nauseated. Mr. Monda was going to feel that because I signed the plea bargaining agreement I was admitting that he was right. I was guilty. Compromised. Dirty. Submitting to legal rape. Mr. Sackey had previously entered a paper to dismiss the case because of the long time involved---three years. But when Mr. Sackey came forward and presented the plea bargain offer, His Honor became visibly upset. He might have been inclined to dismiss as Mr. Sackey had requested. But plea bargaining in this case must have tasted like soured oats to him. I felt an inner quaking at the way he glared at Mr. Sackey.

His Honor asked me if I knew what I was doing, waiving my rights to a fair trial. I could hardly stifle myself. He was making it sound as if I didn't trust him.

I said, "Yes, Your Honor."

Looking steadily at Mr. Sackey, the judge set the sentencing date for January 22. The plaintiff said their recommendation at that time would stand on the recommendation of the probation report.

It took me some time to comprehend that this meant one more extension to leave you dangling,-- the probation report. I was committed to the mercy of a probation officer.

How nice he appeared to be, this young Mexican, Senor Portillo. He claimed to be the nephew of the President of Mexico. He liked flying. He would love to learn to fly. I would love to teach him. The idea of charter trips to Mexico he thought was just great. I should have had enough sense to wonder why, then, wasn't he there under the President's hand operating charter trips all over Mexico. I was to learn that this was baloney to get me to talk, to get absolutely confidential with him and let information and vituperation flow freely.

With my usual gullibility I dump-trucked on him, forgetting he was a domino, told him all my ideas and feelings about the case, what a creep Mr. Monda was, what I thought of the whole bureaucratic system plus the justice system. He smiled. He took notes, pages and pages of notes in shorthand. "This will be easy," he said. "You make yourself perfectly clear."

"If you want to fly to Mexico," he assured, "we'll have to get permission on the twenty-second."

When Mr. Sackey and I walked into the court room on the 22nd, we felt there was no problem. I had made such a hit with Senor Portillo. "Let me get the probation report," he said as he opened the court room door," and we'll read it."

He got it. He started reading. I could see his countenance disintegrating. "Don't you feel well?" I asked."I can't believe this," he said.

I started reading. It was every word I'd said to young Senor Portillo, taken down in shorthand. Added to that was Senor Portillo's personal opinion of me. I was a hostile, vilifying female who displayed a criminal temperament. If you asked him, he 'd say if there was any way to cut corners, circumvent the law or otherwise deserve having the book thrown at me, I'd jump at the chance. He recommended that the four pending counts be piled on top of the one I plea bargained and I be sentenced to 60 months and $4,000 on each count. Multiplied by five that's twenty-five years and twenty thousand dollars.

I had to hold my head up with both elbows on the table. As the judge came out Mr.

Sackey had to lift me to my feet. He set me back down and as our case was first, Mr. Sackey lit into Senor Portillo and his report. It contained outright lies, he said. That business about the FAA revoking my license, for example, had never been substantiated.

With a dour look on his face, His Honor endured Mr. Sackey's tirade to the finish. When he was through Mr. Sackey sat down, his expression hinting that he had made a lot of noise over next to nothing.

Old Iron Horse started reading the law right out of the book. He sounded self vindicated for being a stickler. Then he pronounced sentence.

I STILL here it in nightmares: The full sentence of five years and $10,000 on each count. The sentences, however, were to run concurrently.

In watching the judge in the courtroom previously, I had concluded that the man did have something of a heart, and now and then tried to be fair. Was he coming down so hard on me because he detested would-be plea bargainers? Maybe it was his way of throwing the fear of the Almighty into me.

I burst into tears and made a dash for the courtroom door. A guard hauled me back. As I stood there, tears overflowing, His Honor explained that he was not through with me.

"I am suspending the sentence," he said, "until you serve ninety days for study in some kind of midway house."

Chapter 21

CHESTNUT HOUSE

AFTER watching "One Flew Over the Cuckoo's Nest" the night before, I felt peculiarly oriented next morning for what lay ahead. It was time to report to the CTC (Community Treatment Center at Long Beach).

Ray drove the car. He sensed my apprehension. He tried to chat cheerfully. "Ray, you're a singer of songs to a gloomy heart," I reprimanded, paraphrasing a proverb I vaguely remembered, the one about cheerful chatter out of place.

We pulled out of Chino Airport and passed the youth correctional facility which I used as a landmark in the flight pattern. Soon I'd be inside a facility looking up at other pilots shooting their touch-and-goes above me.

We drove by Fullerton Airport off the 91 Freeway. What a beautiful sight, a twin Cessna on departure making a left turn with the grace of a swan. I would likely loose all that proficiency, if I ever had the privilege of sitting at the controls again. Passing Long Beach Airport did not help either, as the students were lined up for take-off in sequences on Runway 25 L.

Ray tried to divert me again, and suggested we have lunch before going to the Facility (a last meal, I thought) and he pulled off the freeway into the city of Long Beach to look for a restaurant befitting my sendoff.

"Let's go down and look for the prison on Chestnut Street first," I said, "or I will not be able to eat---maybe less afterwards when I see the bars and chains."

Ray humored me. As we neared the neighborhood and finally located Chestnut Street after much inquiring at neighborhood gas stations, we drove down the street about twelve blocks past the old Spanish style homes--they were small residentials from another era, but nice looking. Finally the homes began to be interspersed with garden apartments and then all apartments.

I was sitting on the edge of the seat waiting for the big building with the high walls when suddenly there it was: 1720 Chestnut. No walls, no bars. It was an apartment house much like a three story Travel Lodge. "My God, Ray, they lock you in those rooms, I wonder how often, if ever, they let you out? I don't see any yard for exercise." "Let's go eat," he said.

"No. Drive around the block. I want to look this over first. I may still want to go back to Long Beach Airport and hop a plane for south of the border." The Cuckoo's Nest still stuck in my mind, vindictive guards and horrible overseers like Mrs. Rayburn and all.

Ray won. We went to a restaurant to order. I ordered a fast vodka gimlet to calm myself, and some perch. The perch might as well have been a piece of inner tube. I had to wash it down with coffee, every bite.

"Well," Ray said, "let's go. I have a lot of things to do today."

I flared, the way he brushed the rest of my life into a waste basket. "You know I don't have to be there for an hour!"

"Might as well report in and see what the rules are, when you can have time off, and that sort of thing. You probably won't be allowed to leave for seven days."

Nobody but an ex-con would mock you with words like "time off" and "leave". I could hear the words of my attorney friend Arthur Black as he said, " If you're not nuts when you go in, you will be when you come out."

We drove up in front of the Cuckoo's Nest (1720 Chestnut Street) one hour early. I said to Ray, "No use carrying everything in until I see what I can have and what I can't ." I had all my books and papers, ready to pour out all my hate and grief and dismay in a monumental saga entitled "Monda the Creep".

When my attorney Mr. Sackey had told me how nice it would be---color TV, tennis courts and golf, I screamed, "I don't have clubs!" After managing a flight school for ten years, being chief pilot, FAA examiner, check-out pilot, chief flight instructor, owner of an airline to Mexico and a freight contract with the Navy, and managing 16 employees, there had been precious little time for golf. As I reflected now , it would have been better golfing for ten years---no bankruptcy, no ruined career, no five-year indictment by the Federal Court.

I ENTERED the front door at 1720 Chestnut Street and was greeted by 44 smiling pearlies from the cheerful face of a black gentleman who introduced himself as Willie Thompson. "We have been expecting you," he grinned with anticipation. "You are our first study and first woman at CTC."

I looked around for the sinister crew. Mr. Thompson introduced me to the only two visible beings, ---"This nice young man is your counselor, Skip Askren. And this lady is Marilyn the clerk."

Skip had me be seated and he explained to me the rules. I couldn't believe it. Instead of confinement, I was shown a nice two bedroom apartment with kitchen and living room. I was given a key. Then a sign-out sheet to come and go. Yes, I could have my car there. I could go to work at my job at Chino Airport as flight instructor.   Could I show the apartment to Ray? Why not? I could see he too was in a daze. He had never heard or seen anything like this in his experience with prisons.

I signed in, took the rule sheet, signed out, and started back with Ray for Chino for my TV and typewriter. Just as we were leaving I met a nice gentleman who said he was maintenance supervisor and occupied apartment Four, next to mine. I was situated between No. 2, the office, and this gentleman, probably for good reason, as I was the only woman among 52 men. I think the staff was relieved that I was not an eighteen-year-old marijuana smoker. Secretly I hoped they would not get any more women, so I would not have to share the apartment and guard my belongings.

As we drove back to Chino I was so grateful I had not hopped a plane and tried to fly over the Cuckoo's Nest. The rule sheet said failure to report would have meant five years without mercy.

I had signed back in for 6 PM and found out later I could have been out till 11.

I packed up my TV and my groceries for the new kitchen and so forth, and called Mr. Sackey with the good news.

Before bedtime I was warned to keep my door locked, and did it so securely with the night lock and barricade that the person doing the bed check that night had to pound the door down to wake me for the check. She explained to me to just use the one lock, so that the check would be a bit simpler.

On the second day I had a "counseling" session with Marilyn. It was more like a get acquainted session. We chatted about Mexico and our pets, while Skip, my counselor, was typing out a report to submit to court on a new program for sentencing of inmates as an alternate to jail term. His program, I thought, was beautiful. It followed the example of the old Bible days where offenders of the law paid back their offense by working. For instance a thief had to work and pay back double to the subject of the thievery.

Chapter 22

DEADLINE

I WAS returning from my first weekend pass, four days because of the Monday holiday, and I turned off the exit from Long Beach Freeway onto Pacific Coast Highway. Then it happened. My car seemed to release a final gasp of power. I coasted uphill far enough to come to a stop on the off ramp. Immediately I collected a line of cars behind me, all with raucous horns and voices. Finally some nice young man and his wife helped me. I got out my battery cables, which I always carried, and after much maneuvering he managed to get his truck next to my car, so we could extend the cables. This did not improve the disposition of the lineup, which now extended back into the Freeway. His wife finally maneuvered them around through the ice plant by the side of the road. My car, however, had little energy and refused to start.

My helper, who was wishing he hadn't stopped, gave me a ride to Chestnut Street. I got out on the opposite side so I would not worry him about having had an "inmate" in his car.

I went inside and tried to call a wrecking service but the phone in the lobby is most popular, and I could see it would not be my turn till after hours. Someone mentioned a wrecking service about a block up. I signed out at 11 PM after explaining my flight.

The service was closed, but they suggested another service about three blocks further. It was about this time that I noticed the characters lingering on the street who were not shall we say inspiring. One big black fellow said "What's uh hurry, mama?" It jolted my mind to what I was doing. I recalled the TV movie I had seen the night before, where a black jacket motorcycle gang had assaulted a car, and taken the female on a wild ride and raped and beat her up. She did not come out in any good shape, and they referred to her as "Mama". I walked faster and talked to myself, "Let discretion guide your tongue and your steps, gal."

There was no service at the other station either. So I went to a phone booth to attempt to call some wrecking service I had written down. While dialing a wrecker truck drove by. I jumped from the booth, left the phone dangling, and hailed him down. He came over and I explained. The call I was making was the service I had hailed. "Hang up the phone, lady, and let's go."

The young driver took me to my car and towed it to the local gas station, which would be open at 7 am. All the way there and back he lectured me about walking the streets in this neighborhood. Next day Skip, my counselor, said he did not like to walk this neighborhood even in daytime.

Government, and no 90-day "study" and what else? Why ever did I not stick to roller skating and my little friend Kerry when we were sixteen?

Chapter 23

SOME BRIGHTER SIDE TO PRISON

"THE CHESTNUT HOUSE", proved to be an oasis, especially for my roomies, the 52 guys who were on their way out. They spent their last six months, more or less, there. It was truly a halfway house, and a marvelous idea to transition prisoners. Some of them had no contact with the outside world for three, four, maybe seven years. And the way things changed even in those days, with gas rationing and the trauma of the Cold War at its zenith, must have been a shock.

The Federal employees were most gracious. They did not have the mentality of jailers. They had empathy for their subjects. I could not, in my ever suspicious mind, figure out if it was because of their newness in their job, or if it was because they did not have the atmosphere of clanking chains and bars. They bent over backwards to help the most crotchety specimen. Every inmate was reviewed for job placement. One fine fellow, Chito, went around Long Beach daily talking to factory managers and other commercial prospects where he might find openings. As you might expect, these were rare. An employer has enough problems without "asking for trouble" with someone already strayed from the straight and narrow. It took a lot of convincing and probably the only incentive to them was the fact that while at Chestnut House the inmates showed they wanted to start life anew. Also, cons were willing to work cheaper than the usual laborer in their trade.

But it was hard. After all, as long as the Government kept a brand on them, how could it expect society to forget? Also, if the Government wanted them rehabilitated, why didn't it put them in jobs itself? It was the kind of static Chito said was always filling his ears.

I may be going into rhapsodies about the concept of the Chestnut House, maybe because it saved me from a 4x8 cell; but there really was success in counseling and helping and transitioning a lot of the prison population. Some, in their length of stay in detention, had become institutionalized. They would, rather than face the cruel prospect of the outside, commit a crime just to go back to prison security.

For the most part the residents of Chestnut House seemed to be appreciative and cooperative. The system had its way of screening out incorrigibles in the first place. There was the usual trouble, of course; somebody got out and got drunk and couldn't get back in time, and had to face the consequences. Most of them, if you didn't know the circumstance, would strike you as being normal residents of a regular apartment complex. Some were obvious drug imbibers. Others were very intelligent. One was a purchasing agent. He, too, might have had a bookkeeper like I had.

Chestnut House, after all being part of the Federal system, was, as I would sardonically put it, totally uncoordinated. I was supposed to go to Terminal Island to take some psychological tests, some academic testing, and a physical. (I had just completed my FAA first class physical three days before entry.)

At Terminal Island they shuffled around for about an hour, looking for the head of the department and of course it was his day off. No one seemed to know what to do with a female in a man's prison. They did manage to find the test room, but no one knew if it was the correct test room, especially since the physical was scheduled right in the middle of the testing period for males. The doctor was not expecting a female, since he had a lineup of 25 guys.

By now I was paranoid. Any test they might have started, mental, psychological or physical, I would have pulled zero. Someone finally made the sane suggestion that they just give the tests over to Chestnut House. After all, the tests were basic, down to time clock and answer sheet, and we had counselors and administrators and just about anything they had at Terminal. About six weeks later it turned out that way, with Skip, my counselor, administering the tests. It took me most of that time to convince them that I could get the records of my physical from my doctor.

Later I was interviewed by a psychologist from Terminal Island named Edith Jean Cooper. She approached me rather cautiously, probably saying to herself, What kind of nut do I have to deal with now? She seemed surprised that I seemed sane. I tried jokingly to tell her that of course to be a pilot you have to be an airhead. She showed no appreciation for hangar humor.

Aside from that we had a nice chat. I reviewed my story, of the VA inspection, the shutdown, Mr. Monda's three year siege, the plea bargain fiasco, and my reason for being here for diagnostic study for 90 days. I gave her the file of my experience and background. This time around, by remembering my unloading on my probation officer, Senor Portillo, and the disaster it brought upon me, I took my first basic exercise in trying to be discreet.

Because she showed interest in me, I asked if I could have another interview with her to hear more about her activities.

"For instance," I said, "I have talks with Marilyn, my female counselor here. One time I asked her if, since I was the only girl, did they engage a special person to bed check me twice a night as the regulations called for. " No, Marilyn had said, she did the checking, not just for me but the 52 other "residents". "You mean you walk into a bedroom and count four bodies in two twin beds? What if they post one behind the door and when you come in he closes the door and they clobber you?"

Marilyn had explained that even though there might be rapists at Chestnut House, they knew the consequences. She did say once in awhile there was some male who was proud of his private manly possessions and displayed himself openly with bed clothing thrown aside. If he made a practice of this all she had to do was report him and they shipped him back to his former joint.

Edith, in turn, told me bed checking was her job too, at Terminal Island. She bed checked 160 prisoners twice each night. To do this she had to walk the length of a long dead-end corridor lined with bunks on each side. There was one little man who persisted in starting up a program of masturbating when she would

101

focus her flashlight his way. She finally reported him, and was followed by a guard who caught his performance. Into solitary he went for a couple of weeks.

"One night," she said, "I came to three of the prisoners in a huddle at the end of the hallway. I didn't have my flashlight and when I stumbled on them it obviously upset them. I made a hasty retreat, you bet I did. One of them followed me to the outer corridor in his underwear. I picked up the phone to make a check in, and he decided rape was not the better part of valor."

Edith Jean never came back.

Chapter 24

JEOPARDY

IT was always delightful to look forward to a weekend. It meant three full days, from Friday morning to Sunday evening. I was on my own, to drive and breathe fresh air.

On Friday I had planned to fly Ray up north where he was looking at a ranch to invest in. His settlement trial on his accident was coming up in about two weeks, and this time he was going to invest his money wisely.

However, I was delayed by Skip. Skip said he had to interview me, as he was writing up my 90 day study.

Once again we went over the case, the whole nine yards: the VA, the airplanes, the plea bargaining. I told him the reason I plea-bargained; the prosecuting attorney and even my attorney and everyone agreed that from now on the pressure would be off--- no more harassment on bankruptcy, on airplane deals or students. The tension plus the monetary hopelessness of fighting all these defenses, had made it appealing.

"Too bad a person like you tried to take that way out," Skip shook his head. He never knew how completely his words washed away all semblance of self-worth I had left.

Why had they hounded me so long? I shook my head. Maybe it was because they had my number. Sooner or later they would catch me red-handed.

That line of thinking had already started to sink in on me. I felt like two persons.

One, the Nickie I used to be, wife of a respected elder and mother of two theocratic sons. The other, the Nickie I was now. A would-be plea bargainer. A compromiser. A few days away from an impending prison sentence which I was positive would spin me off into a raving maniac.

I had forsaken my God and my family. When you pour on the remorse like that you end up in sackcloth and ashes.

I noticed the apprehension in Skip's manner as we talked. When we finished in two hours he warned me: "Take no chances, Nickie. Watch all the rules. All the restrictions. Foul up on the least point and you should know who's out there to get you."

I was profoundly perplexed while driving away and thinking about what Skip said. He knew that at Chestnut House I was a model inmate. I obeyed all the rules strictly, I was not interested in drugs, didn't even smoke, kept my apartment neat, checked in and out promptly, never a problem for anyone. But Skip had sounded foreboding, as though he knew something.

Skip had been checking my flying time schedule closely, almost critically, the past few weeks. His final warning as I had walked out the door really had me baffled. He had told me the story of a prosecuting attorney's setup. A young Jewish boy was found with a very small amount of cocaine on him. He had received a three-month slap on the hand. The FBI did not feel this was adequate. "They set him up," Skip said. "They involved this girl somehow to seduce him and trick him, and they picked him up, and this time he got three years."

What chilled me all the more was that this was one Government representative telling me about another Government representative, two representatives supposed to be working for the same end but in reality working against each other. Skip called it "filling their bag of accomplishments, showing results, making their job performance look productive."

All this raised my emotional temperature as I drove to the airport for Ray. From there we'd have to drive to Corona to pick up the plane. I had invested in this plane just before the handcuffs. It was bringing in a rental from my old friend, Don, and in that way was keeping up the payments.

Since I was late from the interview I asked Ray if he'd prefer to wait till next day and leave early. He decided we ought to drive over to Corona and gas up the plane for an early start in the morning. This gas situation was getting to be a problem at that time, and we had to make sure there was 100 octane fuel available.

We loaded Ray's bags and briefcase and taxied the plane to the pumps. There was this car pulling along under my wing to the left and another under the wing to my right. "What do these fools think they're doing?" I yelled.

"Feds," Ray said.

I saw one of them waving a badge. We were surrounded.

I taxied to the side and shut down the plane. We got out . We were corralled by

Corona police, San Bernardino County investigators, and somebody from the FBI. Drug enforcement men.

They started tearing through the plane and the baggage. And looking more disgusted by the minute.

"By the way," Ray said sarcastically, "anybody have a search warrant?" They ignored him. When they failed to find what they were looking for they huddled in shushed conversation. From what I could gather, this time I had stolen somebody's airplane. Only one person could scheme such a charge, my ex-partner in the plane, Bob Fowler. This guy was the biggest con artist I ever encountered. I had watched him embezzle school funds from the ROP on two programs, faster that the State could shell it out. On his complaint against me, Fowler added the suspicion of possible smuggling. In the heat of my fury in learning all this I recalled how Fowler once told me that Mr. Monda had approached him and urged him to file a complaint against me, threatened him if he didn't and then promised him he would have the airplane we owned free and clear. Just to cooperate. Now Fowler was cooperating.

The plane involved with Fowler was not the plane these men were pawing over now. But apparently they thought it was. Had they had the courtesy to ask a few questions first, they could have spared themselves the trouble of scraping paint from the serial numbers.

"I want to call my lawyer," I told the investigator from the District Attorney's office. He shook his head. I insisted. The only way I was finally allowed to make the call was for him to accompany me to the phone and listen to every word. I called Mr. Sackey and described what was going on. Mr. Sackey in typical attorney style told me not to talk to anyone, but to come in and see him the next day if I got out of jail. He advised me to start making arrangements for bail. The icy shakes came over me listening to him.

I started to tell Ray how to get my bail arranged but the investigator interposed by telling Ray he was going to be arrested too.

"On what charge?" Ray demanded. He'd find out soon enough, he was told.

After two hours of fuming and fussing the Federal police left. Then the FAA decided they had no case. The Corona cops pulled out. The decision to arrest was left to the District Attorney's investigator.

"So," Ray repeated, "what are you charging us with?"

"Come in to the DA's office tomorrow with the papers on the plane," he replied. "Meanwhile the plane is impounded."

Evidently they figured it would take more sophisticated searching to find where we had stashed the drugs. I would cry about the plane later. Right now sweet freedom beckoned. Freedom, at least to pre-arrange my bail.

Saturday I met with Mr.Sackey. Monday we appeared before the District Attorney. Mr. Sackey meant to muzzle me. "Just keep quiet. Let them arrest you."

"Keep quiet---Let them arrest you!" I shouted so deep in my throat it came out a whisper. "How can you lawyers shrug your shoulders and tell your client there's nothing to it---like taking a shower!"

"You'll be out in half an hour."

In my estimation no Federal domino ever wiped his nose in half an hour. "I'd like to see every lawyer in the world locked up, and you along with them, for just one day. Then see how glib you'd be about my going to jail."

He thought that was funny.

Ray decided with Mr. Sackey that I should keep my mouth shut. Without an attorney Ray remained silent himself, except that he did tell the DA that if he could have a look at the charges he might have some idea how to answer them.

So we read the complaint. It was signed by Fowler, charging embezzlement and possible smuggling. The complaint was made on a State level. Had it been filed on the Federal level, there would have been the plea bargaining fiasco and other details to cause them some annoyance. I could not believe it. But there it was.

THAT night when I went back to Chestnut House I was expecting the worst. Anybody with any problem, big or small, could be sent back to the prison they came from. Since I came from none, they could send me wherever a domino chose.

I walked in the office, with my card to be signed in and there sat my friend Gretchen.

"You're not going to like this," she began, "but I'll give it to you straight."

My heart thudded so hard I sank down in the chair in front of her.

"What---" I faltered.

"You are not going to like this but I am going to have to do it." Oh God, no psychologist could have taught this dumb female to twist the knife like this. "You are going to have to have a UA."

"A U-what?"

A screen fell down in front of my eyes and a horror movie started unreeling.

"I have to get a sample of urine," Gretchen explained. "I know you don't take drugs or anything, but it's a regulation for everyone here."

Never in my life, and that was years ago, have I been so relieved.

"No problem," I said in a weak whisper.

She pulled from a box a small bottle with a pill in it and said, "Fill it."

"This," I said, studying the bottle, "does pose a problem---somewhat I mean."

"Oh?"

"The quarter inch diameter. I don't know how even the fellow handle this."

"You will have to manage," Gretchen sounded impatient. "I have to leave here in twenty minutes. Appointment."

107

I made a valiant effort, with Gretchen coaching and hurrying. But I missed the whole bottle.

"I have to get out of here on time," Gretchen insisted.

"OK. But my kidneys were never trained to respond on demand. What if I can't produce? You should have forewarned me."

"Fill the bottle," Gretchen said, "or I'll have to write you up as a dirty UA."

I thought of a couple of dirty words for her.

"I just got here," I reminded.

"And I'm just leaving here. With or without the bottle."

I walked over to the sink. I swallowed five glasses of water. If there's anything I detest it's chlorine water. The chlorine, for all I knew, would show up in the test.

My kidneys cooperated. I handed the bottle to Gretchen.

"Have you taken any medication in the last twenty-four hours? If you have it will show up in the test."

"No," I said. "But I'm in need of medication now."

I UNDERSTOOD the bitterness of my fiend Jim Freeborn when he was flying in Mexico. He had drugs planted on his plane. They hauled him in. Four and a half years he fought to get him out. But the Mexican principle, according to Jim, is to hang on to you so long as you have any money left. His wife in the States hocked everything to get him out. They seem to have an uncanny sense of knowing when the last dime has been squeezed, then they let you go. "It is called paying the full ransom or *mordiva*," Jim would say.

Maybe I wasn't headed for a Mexican prison, but I shared the frustration and bitterness Jim felt, and wished, in my heart, I could vaunt my spleen on my persecutors the way Jim and some of his buddies did. When Jim, the ex-con, came to work at Chino Airport, Mr. Monda was on his back, constantly. Jim was tough. The names he called Mr. Monda filled every other word in a sentence, and would make the Devil cringe. Jim and his buddies worked up such a rage against Mr. Monda; they knew the phone was tapped, so they would call each other and plan a humongous push. When a posse of agents would burst in on them, there they'd be playing cards in pure innocence. "Why don't you (deletion) go after some kindergarten, you sure as (swear word) won't go after the Mafia---You'd get your (blankety-blank) heads blown off." Then they'd say to each other, "Look at these (scorcher) freaks, pulling down taxpayers salaries. These (ear burner) jerks couldn't follow a baby with a dirty diaper." Jim would say, "My Congressman couldn't believe how stupid you are. So he's come along and he's listening in the next room. You don't believe it? Go in and introduce yourself."

That night in the dark of my room, I lay on my bed and thought how I'd like to light in to these people with a venom and hatred such as Jim Freeborn himself had not tasted. But that was the very spirit that had roiled in my veins all these years. I tried to take stock. I had a talk with myself. "Nickie, this kind of thing, look where it got you. Is it because you're as stubborn as the Devil? The people you set up to take over your air flights to Mexico are now flying regular routes and making good. You have not flight service. You're bankrupt. All you have is a claim to one impounded airplane and maybe a few loyal students. Why do you keep hanging on? Even a goat knows when to stop butting the wall."

Of course I might not have to be concerned about staying on. The five-year sentence hanging over my head could settle it all. With clipped wings I could not fly. If I could not fly I could not live.

Chapter 25

NICKIE RANTS, EUNICE PRAYS

THE big day was coming up at Chino Airport, the annual EAA Airshow. With the Show coming up I was planning to earn some desperately needed bucks. An idea popped in mind. Every day during lunch time two wagon venders made the rounds of the Air Port with their sandwiches and sweets and drinks and so on. I still held the lease on the area where my apartment and trailer were located.

Why not make a deal with the vendors, say, on a 20% commission, and station them out there full-time for the two days? Jerry, one of the vendors, went for it. I got the permits and made the big plans and bought some airplane balloons and sunglasses and straw hats with my last dollars, to double my profits.

Came Friday, the day before the show. Up drove the canale truck and Jerry hopped out. "I've got bad news. We can't do the show." He was crushed. "The head of the show and county director Jeets said no go. Only Air Race personnel can handle concessions.'

"Are they telling me I can't do as I please on my own leased property?"

"All I know is they told my boss Jerry if we do this the trucks will never be allowed on the Airport again and our lease will be canceled. I'm sorry. Jerry said tell you no go."

That left me with a bunch of balloons and sun goggles. My pals, Don and Pixie, came down to help me set up the tables and display. Then we sat down for coffee as we surveyed the prospects. That's when a hot-dog truck pulled up and parked directly in our entrance.

I lost my cool. "These (Jim Freeborn language) can't do this." Over I went to the EAA headquarters and exchanged some unprintables with the head cheese, Fred Broun. "Get that ... truck out of my entrance---and I mean now!"

110

"I have a contract for this airport," he said. "Nothing is moving."

"I'll give you thirty minutes---no, twenty minutes or blow the (excuse) hot-dog hawker sky-high."

"Call the Marines."

On the way back I ran into the airport manager and even though he filtered his eyes with his lashes every time he looked at me, the mood I was in intimidated him, I think. Even he agreed it was wrong to blatantly block the entrance. By that time four sheriff's cars had driven up and parked, looking around for the wild woman about to blow a truck away. One deputy got out, confused by the lack of action. "This truck is illegally parked," he said. "Who's responsible for this?"

At that precise moment Fred Broun drove up. "There he is now," I pointed. The cop dashed up to Broun's car and read him the riot act for illegal parking. Pixie and I snickered till we rattled our coffee cups. The cop never did understand that Broun had called him to stop me from blowing the truck away.

Next morning the hot-dog truck did not reappear. Broun spent half the day calling the Airport officials with his complains. Evidently they did not want any more invasions by the sheriff's posse. We went on with our sales and made some bucks, though not as much as hoped for. The show as a whole was a failure. I would have sacrificed my investment for a downpour to wipe the whole thing out.

Within two days I had two inspections from the Environmental Health Department., at the request of the Airport. The EHD pinned on my door at Building 1112 a notice of cancellation of my lease.

As I drove the freeway that night to Chestnut House I told myself out of spite against the whole world, "There's got to be some joy in this plight. But what is it?"

At the same time something deep within kept whispering "You're fighting the world with its own weapon, the spirit of the world. It's bigger than you. You'll never win."

Someone once said, "Take courage! I have conquered the world." But my war was not His war.

111

Gretchen had another announcement waiting for me: "You have a room mate now."

This is the end, so help me God. She's already pawned my typewriter, my TV. Now I don't even have privacy from harassment. Thought like that sizzled as I rammed headlong through the door. I found here in the other bedroom, flipping her Bible, 250 pounds of black female.

"You must be Nickie," she said cheerily. "I'm Eunice."

Four hours later we were still talking. I think I received in those four hours more entertainment than TV has put out since its inception.

Eunice described for me in vivid detail her incarceration, her treatment at the hands of the dominos, punctuated every few minutes by a prayer of thanks for her salvation that had carried her through the ordeal. Her crime, from what I could piece together, had to do with how she initialed and signed some W2 forms and checks, all masterminded by her brother, while he was in prison or between sentences. It seemed her husband, "Ole Solomon", was also in Chestnut House for his part in the tax caper.

Eunice had her downs with an FBI woman who could have been Mr. Monda's wife. "Same dirty tricks and nasty grin and lordin' oveh you, like you says, Honey."

One time she threw the female FBI woman bodily out of her house. I wagged a finger at Eunice and said, "That was no fun because these clinkers don't bounce." She nearly rolled off the bed.

Her description of her arrest and stay at Sybil Brand was right out of a Chinese prison camp. They handcuffed her behind her back. It was no easy task stretching here arms around the backside of that girth of hers. At Sybil Brand they herded her down a corridor and a voice over the loudspeaker, out of sight somewhere, directed her to march. The prison doors opened electrically and she was directed by the voice down another corridor with no lights, black as herself, and a pencil point of light shined on the number on her cell door, and she was directed by the voice to enter the door, on the double, in the pitch dark. The door clanged shut behind her, cold steel slamming cold steel.

The voice, still helpful, told her to feel around and climb the ladder to the top bunk. First, she bumped into the commode, which filled the 18 inches of space between the end of the bunk and the wall. Anyway, the ladder did not come apart and she climbed up and squeezed herself into the 18 inches of space above the bunk. Eunice measured off 18 inches from the tip of her middle finger to her elbow. Then she dropped her elbow on the bed by her side, her fingers pointed upward, to show me that her middle ballooned higher than the tips of her fingers. She sent up a prayer that she was not claustrophobic, and that her head was at least not on a level with the commode.

The mattress was as thin as a chaise lounge cover. For days the marks of the springs were imprinted on her body. She was not allowed to sleep because every few hours the Voice directed her to climb down and to walk back through the dark corridor to the entrance door and stick her arm through the bars so they could read her arm band number. On one of these trips she was made to stand thirty minutes without touching any wall in the dark and if she leaned on one hip or shifter her weight the Voice would scream at her to straighten up. This was not helped by her cell mate who chided the Voice and that only kept Eunice standing there even longer.

Her description of the booking left not much room for human dignity. They gave her a gown so short her rear end stuck out when she moved. She was sprayed from every angle and in every crevice with DDT and checked for bugs.

The gal inmates were hard. They propositioned her. She held her cool. She put on a tough act. They didn't tackle her.

She described one nice looking young woman who had just entered the holding tank, looking a bit timid, and lamenting how her boyfriend was off making out with a neighbor. She was attacked by one of the lessies who was all over her, from head to toe. Nobody came to her aid, but watched as though this was a common sight, which it was.

The prostitutes, she said, were all the time bragging and gloating over their exploits. One time the guards brought in a couple whom they termed "dykes". The guards said "We'd better not put the dykes in there with the others. At that same time they pulled Eunice out to go to court. She never learned what dykes meant.

Her husband, Ole Solomon, she said, was worse than a nervous wreck. He wrote out a financial statement for the judge. While he was fanning himself with the paper she looked at it and saw he had put down that they owned a '79 Volkswagen and they never owned a Volkswagen. If she hadn't corrected that, they would have been paying a big fine.

Eunice gave the judge a lecture about her experiences, her loss of outside dignity, being put in jail, and she told him if she was sentenced to one of "them women's' prisons" she would have no inside dignity left either, and then he would have something on his conscience. She lectured about the whole episode, the chase, the arrest, the treatment in jail, and pleaded with the judge to show mercy. It either worked or she wore him out. She was sentenced to Chestnut House for six months. Solomon was here for 90 days.

After they left the court they drove home, and while there the phone rang. It was the CTC, wanting to know where they were, and they had better get right down here now, or else. She woke Solomon who was over-fatigued and sacked out on the couch. "You better wake up, Solomon. Else you is gonna sleep you'self right into prison. They thinks we has excaped."

She got Solomon up and right to Chestnut House they came and checked in. They, of course, requested an apartment together. "No," Gretchen said, "we can't have any sex here."

"You no need worry about that, Ma'am. Ole Solomon he ain't that lively nohow. " Anyway they were assigned different quarters. And since Solomon worked nights and she worked days...well, it was a pretty jumbled tale, told in about the sequences I tried to follow.

Chapter 26

THE INCREDIBLE HAUCK

AS my 90 days wound down my nervous system developed ulcers of terror at times. I would wake up in a lather of sweat pounding the face of the man who brought me to ruin, only it turned out to be a pillow. That's how leery I was yet of Mr. Monda. Surely he could not influence Marilyn or Skip. Skip had even requested a transfer from the California prison system because he could not help rehabilitate prisoners the way he wanted to. Marilyn and Skip so loudly disclaimed the entrapment methods used by the FBI that I was edgy about whether they might discredit themselves in the judge's estimate. He was, after all, the domino who would decide. If His Honor was consulting with dominos behind the scenes he was getting reports as fare apart as north is from south.

Mr. Sackey called. "I guess," he said nonchalantly, "my secretary called and told you we are to be in court tomorrow at l:30 for sentencing."

I picked my heart up off the floor. "No," I said, "Your secretary told me nothing."

"I could not get the report," he added, after a pause. "We will just have to read it when we get there."

I could tell that he was nervous. Maybe he viewed the prospects with mixed feelings. On one hand he might hope the judge would dismiss the whole thing and he, Sackey, would be relieved of me. On the other hand, this mess could be prolonged into the next generation and it was obvious I was not one of his lucrative clients.

Back at the apartment I tried to bolster my nerves with a fortification of bourbon and soda. In a bleary, pre-execution state of mind, I gathered up whatever files I thought might be helpful.

No way was I going to leave my fate totally in the hands of an attorney.

Not that I would be leaving anything behind. All my facilities were canceled. If my job at the airport was still open, the drive to Long Beach was no longer feasible. The fuel crunch was really on at that time in the US. The lines were becoming two and three hours long at gasoline stations.

What a blessing it would have been to spend a few hours in a plane, soothing my spirits, soaring above the green earth . Always it meant a lift above mundane matters, regardless of how dire their enormity. Up there, out of reach of the moral pollution , you had vertical, one-to-one relationship with a God of mercy, and help to lift you beyond all distress---that is, if you had a relationship with Him. The nearest I could get to Him was a wooden bench to sit on and stare at the judge's podium and wonder where has the freedom gone?

But all was not bleak as Tartarus. I had met my lawyer Mr. Sackey, on the courthouse steps. He had the report from Chestnut House. We hurried into the library to read it.

"Wait a minute," I said, "Only three pages long? It took 90 days to write that? At tax payer's cost each page is worth a fortune."

"It's short and sweet," Mr. Sackey said.

It was. I suspected it was good. I was portrayed as cooperative, cheerful, a person who chatted freely about my case. Seemingly I depended on and trusted other people too much to tend to my business affairs, and that was my downfall. I had even ignored my legitimate claim to $26,000 of earned FAA fees. The report did not mentioned that I had hired an ex-con. At any rate they said I had no psychotic problems, was "normal". They did not recommend any sentencing, perhaps short term counseling, if anything at all. Dear good old Skip. Even Mr. Sackey was happy.

"Nothing derogatory here for me to refute," Mr. Sackey declared.

"The judge may come up with some," I reminded.

Now court was coming to order. Everybody stood up. His Honor entered. He sat down and rapped. Everybody sat down.

This was it. My hands were sweating and my mouth was as dry as cotton.

His Honor explained: Due to the gas shortage several of the judges were not able to get here. The head judge, by the way, had just retired. "So," he actually smiled, "the Incredible Hauck has added responsibilities." "Oh Lord," I thought, "that's his name---Judge Hauck, and that's his diabolical way of letting us know he's going to be Diablo in a black robe."

The room was packed with people. I whispered to Mr. Sackey that he wouldn't get to us till Juvember. As it turned out most of the people were creditors on the appeal of actor Lee Marvin's palimony case, and they were dismissed to come back at four o'clock. The first case heard brought up this little Mexican wetback. It seemed he had a mania for sneaking across the border to get the good US. pay scale. As soon as he got a pay day he'd get drunk or high on something and take off in a friend's car. He did not whip it across the border and sell it, but would merely abandon it. When he sobered up he'd go about his way. The car meanwhile would be reported stolen. Zap, he'd go to jail. Ten times this had happened. This time he'd been in jail nine months waiting trial and he had been beaten by guards and other inmates. He was in Federal court this time on a charge of being an alien illegally across the border. His court appointed attorney pleaded with the judge to recommend some psychiatric help. At twenty-four this young man did not seem to learn lessons well.

His Honor was humane. He talked to Pedro through an interpreter. He appointed him eighteen months at LOMPBOC for treatment.

"United States Vs Johnson," the clerk intoned. The elephant was about to trounce the mouse.

Up we got. "Don't say anything," Mr.Sackey warned me. "Let me do the talking.

All the talking."

"I just want to make a couple of statements---"

"No---"

The Incredible Hauck interrupted. "Do you have anything to say, Mrs. Johnson?" Then he interrupted himself. "Before you

117

say anything, let me tell you what I've decided. I have read your report, and the letters from people you worked with, who know you, and everything seems to be complimentary. I have gone over the background of your situation, Mrs. Johnson. Attempts have been made to bring various charges against you. None of them appear valid. The VA, for example, never found any valid fault with you or your school. Neither did the SBA. The one charge that you plea bargained was for the sale of a plane which was not even yours, and which the SBA could hold no lien on, was in fact your husband's and your son's. Anyway, the long and short of it is, I am dismissing your case."

I started to speak. Mr. Sackey put his hand over my mouth. "We'll accept that, Your Honor---Gladly!"

"What do you mean--We?" I bit his finger. I wanted to release a flood of frustrations. Sackey was practically dragging me out of the courtroom.

Outside the courthouse we paused. I closed my eyes. I breathed the deepest sigh of my life. It had been six months since Mr.Monda placed his hand on my shoulder and grinned icily.

We all---Sackey and Pixie and Don and Ray---went down to Chinatown for a little saki.

Chapter 27

THAT OTHER PART OF LIFE

THAT night I drove out alone for one last look at Chino Airport. As I cruised across the grounds I paused in front of the old flight school that looked like a haunted hangar of inactivity. Here I had trained hundreds of grateful pilots. Bruce now had the hangar to himself and was successfully modifying P51's, jets and large aircraft. I remembered how he had started with us in a corner of the hangar with a phone on the floor beside his one airplane. Meadowlark was going strong training pilots I had to forfeit when I lost the VA account. There were the three brothers I had trained, setting them up in their own business which I named for them, "Cal Aire". I had carried their account until they got started selling aircraft. I passed Steve Hinton's headquarters. He started taking lessons in a Piper Cub, and from there I gave him his commercial check ride in a P51. He had flown a Red Baron to first place in the air races and was now the most successful young air race participant in the sport.

.Two other businesses were centered at this airport, two with whom I held a special bond. Air Cortiz owed its existence to its first passengers furnished by me, and to the use of my Mexican Air Permit for its first flight to Baja. The other operation, San Carlos Bay, picked up the operation I could not follow through because of my 90- day wonder course.

"More power to all of you," I said to the silent grounds.

It was a bittersweet farewell. You don't console yourself with complete relish, thinking you're the pioneer paving the way for others to flourish where you have failed. I halted in front of my little "white house" still surrounded by the chain fence to keep out the Mondas. That, too , had failed. There was no staying here tonight or ever again. The letter of eviction was still nailed to the door.

That morning as I sat in that courtroom awaiting the verdict of a man who held my life in his hands, I vowed that if I ever got out of this mess I would turn my life around as it had never been turned before.

Now I was free. I was not a person promising God I would reform if He would only save me from this trial. No, at last I was simply free to choose. This was how it should be. I was free to turn of my own will, in the right direction. If there was any way to find God's forgiveness for my willfulness, my waywardness, I must find it. Whatever it took to find the humility of spirit, a courage not of compromise, I would not stop breathing till I found it. I did not want merely to go back to my former years of serving the true God of happiness. I had not been truly happy myself. Everything was conditional then on wings first and God, husband and family second. This had to be reversed. Exactly reversed.

Not that there was something wrong with love of flying. What was wrong was being obsessed, mastered by it. I wanted what David wanted, after he went astray in the affair of Bathsheba: "Create in me a new heart, O God, and put within me a new spirit, a steadfast one". The words broke through the pall that blinded me. For the first time I felt there was hope for me. David, after taking Uriah's wife and getting him killed, had a lot to ask forgiveness for, but he knew God's mercy was there: "The sacrifices to God are a broken spirit; a heart broken and crushed O God, you will not despise."

It was time I headed for the Ozarks. So much of my life had slipped away, I would hardly recognize my three granddaughters and my new grandson, Joel. It was time to make up for that other part of life. Swede, faithful Swede, was there. It was not too late, I hoped and prayed, to make up for that part I really never shared with him.

THREE GENERATIONS OF PILOTS

JOHN, 16, WITH INSTRUCTOR NICKIE

BRANDI, 16, AFTER SOLOING

SURROUNDED BY GRANDCHILDRED,
SWEDE, IN FINAL DAYS OF
LOU GEHRIG DISEASE

HAY RIDE IN THE OZARKS

MISSOURI HORIZONS

Chapter 28

HOME

I WAS coming home with my heart in my mouth. What would it be like in the Ozarks? How would my family receive me? Would they understand my change of heart?

From out of the smoggy, smelly Los Angeles basin you ascend beyond it all, and after a few hours you descend to a green earth under crystal-blue skies. In every direction you're enchanted by the pure snow of blooming dogwoods, the fuchsia haze of redbud trees, the fragrance of honeysuckle, and distantly you glimpse a little lake sparkling like sapphires. Springtime in the Ozarks.

But how will they greet you? Out of this paradise setting come your people, your family, your beloved ones, the ones you abandoned these so many years. It was nerve-shattering to anticipate.

Each and every one seemed born right out of this blessed spot. Swede was gracious. In his 50's, he had matured amiably. He took me to his mobilehome in a beautiful park where there was uncrowded space and a swimming pool, a golf course and best of all, an airstrip. I looked out and fairly trembled with ecstasy, over smooth trimmed grass thousands of feet to the edge of the drop to Table Rock Lake.

And my children! John and Sam and their wives paraded my grandchildren, three sweet cuddly girls and one squirmy boy. Grand-parenting, oh it's wonderful, with protective parents waiting to take over---the frosting on the cake of parenting.

Swede, in his maturity, was more than ever a handsome hunk. He courted me, took me out to dinner and showed me the countryside, the tourist attractions of Eureda Springs, Ark, and Silver Dollar City. There was something reminding us of when we first met so long ago in a war- torn world, but now we were falling in love in that now-and-forever way I had missed till now.

I could see us settling down to a semi-retirement state, enjoying our houseboat on the lake, exploring the fingers of water weaving in and out of the Ozark hills. And there were flights in the Cessna l50, part-time as an instructor, and trips in the Piper Comanche that I had salvaged from California. And in the evening the peace and quiet of a twilight aglow with the rhythmic glimmer of fireflies.

Beautiful to a point. I was still a disfellowshipped person. My family had taken me in when I had no place else to go, the prodigal coming home. Even with them I could not share spiritual acceptance. The little congregation was gracious, wanting to enfold me, but the barrier was there. My husband and my two stalwart sons were elders. My two daughters-in-law were pioneers (60 to 90 hours a month in the public ministry) several months out of the year. I had to be the black sheep. My family did not deserve this.

I lost no time approaching the elders, asking to be reinstated. It was an awkward arena for those few elders who were not related to me, and who had to meet with me. What a test on them, having to deal with the disfellowshipped wife and mother of the Johnson family! Yet, "There is no partiality with God"!-- Romans 2:11.

The meetings began. I felt repentant. Truly repentant. I was sorry, but sorry for what? For not appreciating sacred things? Or sorry for the inconvenience and reproach of being a person cut off from spiritual fellowship with my family and friends? I wondered myself, along with the elders, if I still had some of the spirit of Esau. Esau, the twin brother of Jacob, showed callous disrespect for Jehovah's arrangements when he sold his divinely bestowed birthright to his brother for a bowl of stew. Later Esau wept bitterly, not because of a repentant spirit toward God, but because his father Isaac would not restore the birthright to him. Esau at no time showed appreciation for sacred things. What he regretted was the loss of a birthright inheritance that had become valuable to him. I wondered if to some extent the loss of prestige of being the wife and mother of a family in fine standing weighed more in my remorsefulness than anything else. The elders sensed my soul-searching. They considered it a sign of true repentance toward Jehovah. I was reinstated.

I entered into the joy of being a member of the Cassville congregation. It was a warm and friendly spiritual community, happy and free from so many city pressures. A new life in every sense, with a new horizon, for me.

THE ministry service in this area was refreshing. Everywhere you meet a car or pickup people waved. "Who was that?" I'd ask Swede. "I don't know," he'd answer. "Here everybody waves at you."

People were hospitable. This was the fringe of the Bible Belt. Few people were searching for the real meaning of God's word. They were satisfied with the hoary teachings handed dowr to them through generations. They had , in some hazy fashion, some concept of a Trinity, a hellfire (this latter a convenience I think they felt was ready-made for us ".no-hellers"), and a few shredded doctrines; but the main thing seemed to be that if you "accept Jesus" and are maybe "born again", that's all that's necessary. You have your spiritual insurance policy, good for a golden harp and a cloud to sit on in glory land.

For the most part when we knocked on their doors or caught them in the cow barn, they smiled congenially and listened courteously and you'd think they were ready to invite you in and start a home Bible study. Then they would smile and say, "I wouldn't be interested."

Most of our territory was rural. We would drive down long winding dirt roads, and eat our lunch by gentle streams in the woods. The beauty was marred only by ticks and chiggers. "You think we'll be tormented by these little monsters in Paradise?" "We've got a lot to learn about Jehovah's creation." Then everybody would laugh and scratch harder

When it was rainy you'd sometimes get stuck in the mud in the middle of nowhere. Usually somebody would come along to help. Many a brother's suit went to the cleaners after those trips. My sons and their wives, who'd pioneered the area for years, had every experience imaginable.

SWEDE had turned into a true Ozarkian. There was no such thing as rush. He was totally content with the fishing and hunting without the city pressures. He had bought himself a shop on three acres called Grandpa's Workshop. He was making signs with wooden letters, small antique cars (he could never leave his love for cars far behind), and as an afterthought to please me, small twin engine oak airplanes. It was his delight to piddle in the shop. His work was a credit to his cabinet-maker father who had come from Sweden at 12, speaking only Swedish, and made it way up in the ranks of Peerless Motor Car Company. Swede also had bought an old Model T Ford to restore in the future.

It looked as though we were finding our happiness transitioning quietly and happily into the "golden years", encouraging our family as their children grew up in "the discipline and mental-regulating of Jehovah". Our hearts were gladdened to help others turn from the hopelessness of an old world to the bright horizons of an incoming new world of everlasting life.

But then, as the wise man said, time and unforeseen occurrence befall us all. It was on a trip to an outdoor drama called "Shepherd of the Hills" that I realized something was wrong with Swede. During one part of the play they had a barn dance and persons from the audience were invited down to the stage. Swede always loved to dance, especially to this type music and polkas. I tried to pull him on the dance floor, but he said he could not dance. What had happened to this lover of music? I thought he had a momentary charley horse, like the ones he seemed to experience at night.

Then a few days later a small fire started in the trees outside the woodshop. We all ran to the fire and called to Swede to hurry with a bucket of water. He could not run; just walk. Something was definitely wrong.

I convinced him to make an appointment at the VA Medical Center in Kansas City. Following our circuit assembly in St. Louis, we took him to the Center.

It would happen at a time like this when an ogre from out of the past rose to haunt me. I got a call from Arthur Samuel Black II, a Los Angeles attorney and one of my former students.

"It's about your friend, Ray Bell, Nickie," he said. "We're trying to settle for Workmen's Compensation. It's been hanging fire since his fall off the bus in Mazatlan. We can't settle it without you. Can you come out?"

No, I could not, not with Swede's condition hanging over us.

"No problem," Arthur said. "We'll just come out there and take depositions. I've always wanted to see the Ozarks."

One thing outstanding in the Ozarks at that time was a black man. Art was blacker than a black cat in a coal mine at midnight. He and Ray came out. We had many meetings with my local attorney. I took Art flying and showed him some of the scenery.

In this community, such a thing as a white woman taking a black man flying received notoriety.

After a week of tests Swede came home. The news was like a death blow. He was diagnosed with A.L.S. (Amatrophic Lateral Sclerosis) commonly known as Lou Gehrig Disease. From that date, July 1980, the degression set in. First in the legs; then the arms and hands.

Also, from this time my problems with the elders started all over again. Ray Bell was still a disfellowshipped person. In my meetings with Art and Ray and my attorney, there were the inevitable luncheon breaks. Now the elders were not making a mountain out of the issue, but---

"But," they tried to explain, "Sister Johnson, it kind of puts us on the spot." What troubled them was the principle involved in the apostle Paul's first letter to the Corinthians, in chapter five, having to do with mixing with anyone representing himself as a brother when he definitely is not one---"not even eating with such a man".

"Aren't you straining out a gnat and swallowing a camel?" I retorted. Ray was not proclaiming himself a brother. "To begin with," I said, "he was baptized without really knowing what dedication was all about. He was not dedicating himself to Jehovah. He said he got baptized so the friends who studied with him would feel they had not wasted their time. His relationship with the Witnesses was over a long time ago."

I resented their trumping me at a time of such great anxiety.

"The problem is," they explained patiently, "If we are to help such a person we must not give him the impression that disfellowshipping is a light thing to be overlooked."

I could have shown a little humility and asked the brothers for help. In a way, they were asking me for help. When *do* you consider a disfellowshipped person no longer one to treat as such? What would have been the impact on Art Black and the other lawyer if I had said "I can't have lunch with you if Ray is around"?

The one thing on my mind was that my husband was doomed to certain paralysis and death.

SUDDENLY the green was gone from the Ozarks. I was back in that bleak world of stress and anxiety and relentless tensions. Although Art Black and Ray Bell were gone, these meetings were not. Ingrained in my system from years in civil and criminal courts was the adversary attitude. These brothers were putting me on trial at the sorest moment. They were judges, not shepherds, not counselors. Their objective was to condemn and expel me, not recover me like a straying sheep. That's the way I viewed things. I explained nothing. "Let them prove intent" were lawyer words ringing in my ears.

Once again I found myself telling the elders, "I'm sick unto death of this. Do what you have to do." I walked out.

I was disfellowshipped a second time for the same rebellious spirit. What I had done was right in my eyes. Right or wrong was not so much the issue as who was the rightful determiner. It was not in me at the time to appreciate that if everybody in the congregation took that attitude, there would be no willingness to agree or to acknowledge that Bible principles, if allowed to prevail, could have resolved the issue. If my spirit prevailed in every one there would be nothing new nor different about the Bible-based society of Jehovah's people.

Again I sank into the old pit of anger and bitterness, and that martyred state of going it alone.

Swede, meanwhile, degressed rapidly. It haunts me still that what happened to me might have hastened the end. For him it was first the wheelchair, then loss of use of arms and hands. With the help of a respirator he made it till March 1983. His golden years were not to be. My years were lonely, so very lonely, without my Buddy.

AS I listened to Swede's memorial talk given by Joe Bowling, my mind flashed back to the times when Swede gave such talks to comfort those with loss, and to enlighten those without knowledge of the resurrection. He used the familiar scriptures, such as John 5:28,29, assuring that all those preserved in God's memory "will hear his voice and come out". He cleared the big point of confusion in Christendom, the point having to do with human destiny. Before Jesus the Jews did not expect to go to heaven. After Jesus everybody in Christendom expected to go to heaven or else to hell. The simple truth, as Swede would explain, and as Joe was now saying, is that the physical realm in an earthly Paradise is mankind's destiny.

I could hear Swede reviewing in his warm, compassionate voice, the prophetic blessings of Isaiah 35, how the earth is revived with water in the desert plains, the eyes of the blind are opened, the deaf ones cry out, and the lame climb and leap like the hart. The choice is not heaven or hellfire, but life everlasting or death everlasting.

I moved away to Roger AR to instruct a flight school. It was like Jonah on the ship to Tarshish. I was relieving my family of embarrassment at least. But I was swallowed up in the realization that in all my life I had missed the point. I had never known real humility. It was not a matter of falling down obsequiously before men. I was not now nor ever had been a humble person before my God. Not that all elders were humble either. But there was no benefit in casting blame. What I had to do was contend with the person within. Let others make their own peace with their Maker.

It was that awful, fearsome guilt that King David felt when he admitted his digression with Bath-sheba. "When I kept silent my bones wore out through my groaning all day long. My life's moisture has been changed as in the dry heat of summer."

I let no grass grow under my feet. I asked for a meeting with the Rogers congregation. Letters were exchanged with the Cassville elders. I kept up with the meetings. I studied and engaged in informal witnessing. And I prayed, O God I prayed. I was an old wineskin trying to hold the new wine and it wouldn't work. "Create in me even a pure heart, O God, and put within me a new spirit, a steadfast one." That was my prayer, the prayer of David. Time went by. A year went by. This was still the Ozarks, where time winds down on its own clock. Not many persons are disfellowshipped twice for the same reason. When does such a person truly reform? "Draw close to God, and he will draw close to you." When? That is, when *does* one draw close to God?

I didn't want to be a rebel. I wasn't out to prove I was a liberated female. Eve tried that. She ended up being dominated by a spineless man.

Neither did I want to be a sniveling beggar. "Fear God and keep his commandments. For this is the whole obligation of man." That's what I wanted. The Creator said he created male and female to image Him. That was--that is my aspiration, the grandest aspiration there is for a human made in God's image---reflect His divine love, wisdom, justice and power in your personality. Angels, even his Son, have no higher aspiration.

Another year went by. I did not cast hope aside. Neither did I despair or give vent to bitterness. Something indeed must have changed in Nickie Carter Johnson. The time came when the elders asked me how I really felt. Calmly I quoted the words of Peter to Jesus: "Lord, whom shall we go away to? You have sayings of everlasting life."

Again I was reinstated.

THE years that have gone by since then have been happy ones, restored with my family, here in the Ozarks. I have taught my grandchildren how to fly. I am still flight instructor on a part-time basis. But I am an auxiliary pioneer on a full-time basis. This helps me keep my balance in "seeking first the kingdom and his righteousness." My horizon is higher than manmade wings can reach. It is the lesson I have learned the heartbreak way. An obsession can make you part of this world, and then this world becomes the limit of your horizon.

The world of flying is like the music world, or the arts; it twines itself into your heartstrings. It becomes a love, a way of life. It will leave room for nothing else, and you will defend it with the armor of willfulness. It will leave room for nothing else if you let it. The story of my life.

That is, my past life. I am convinced heart and mind that Jehovah's people see history in its true light, guided by the prophecies of the Word of Life. There is no greater service to mankind than to announce the best news that ever reached this earth. We are on the brink of a new system, the long awaited Kingdom of God.

The End